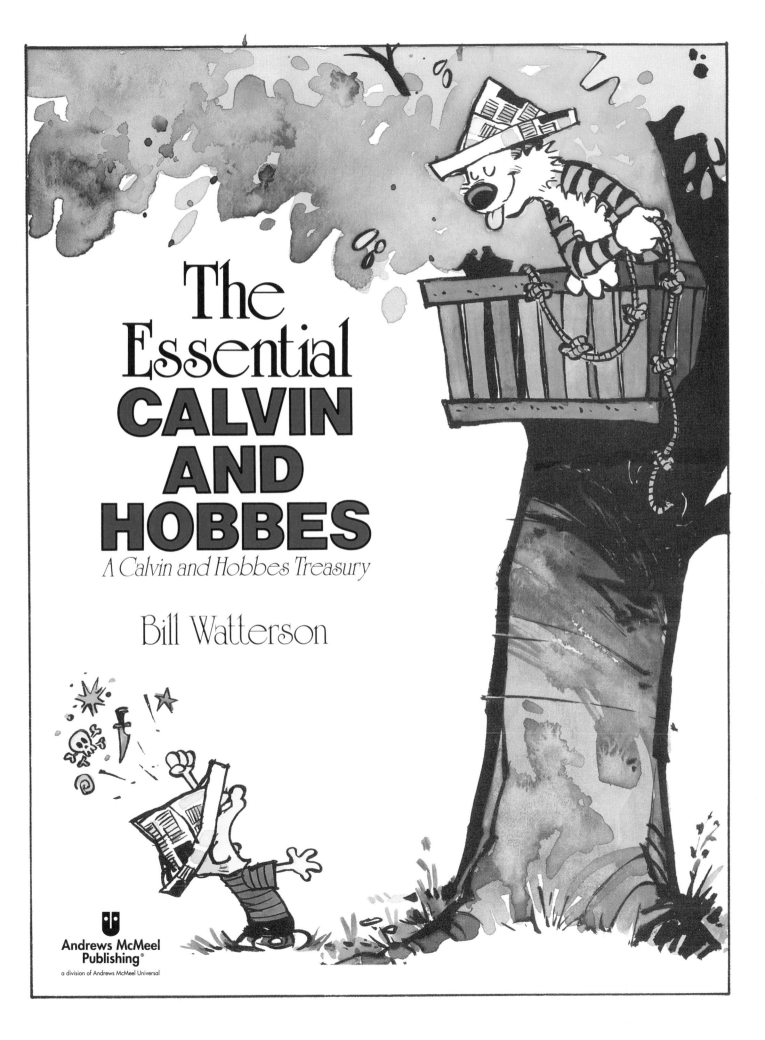

Andrews McMeel Publishing
a division of Andrews McMeel Universal
1130 Walnut Street, Kansas City, Missouri 64106

www.andrewsmcmeel.com

ISBN: 978-1-4494-7233-7

Library of Congress Control Number: 88-71105

22 23 24 25 26 SDB 10 9 8 7 6 5 4 3

Foreword

B ill Watterson draws wonderful bedside tables. I admire that. He also draws great water splashes and living room couches and chairs and lamps and yawns and screams, and all the things that make a comic strip fun to look at. I like the thin little arms on Calvin and his shoes that look like dinner rolls.

Drawing in a comic strip is infinitely more important than we may think, for our medium must compete with other entertainments, and if a cartoonist does nothing more than illustrate a joke, he or she is going to lose.

Calvin and Hobbes, however, contains hilarious pictures that cannot be duplicated in other mediums. In short, it is fun to look at, and that is what has made Bill's work such an admirable success.

— Charles M. Schulz

To Tom

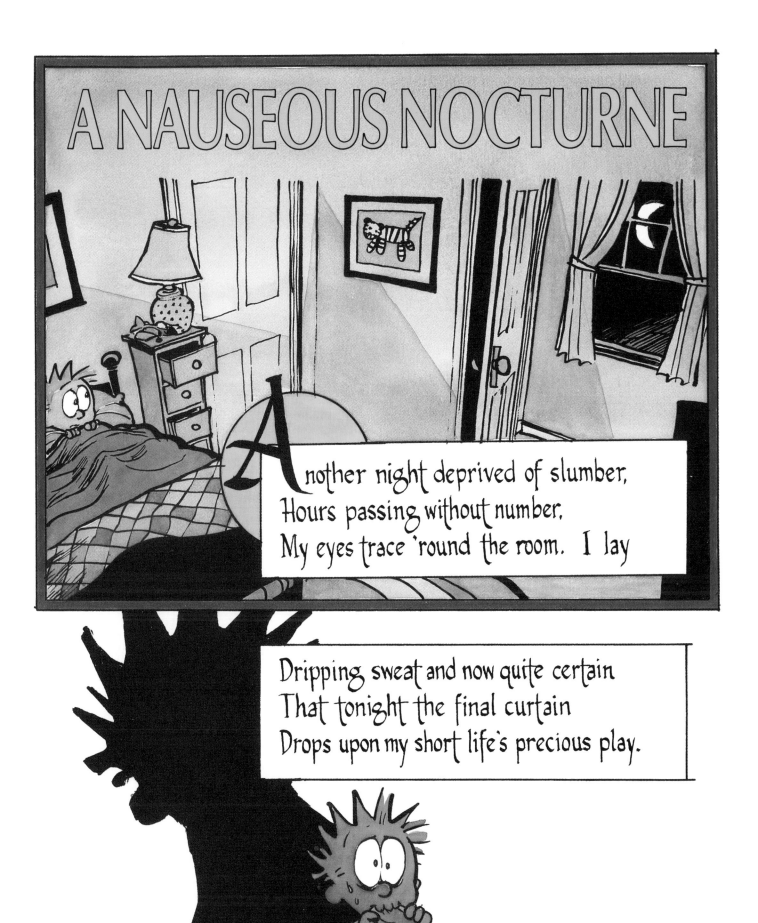

A NAUSEOUS NOCTURNE

Another night deprived of slumber,
Hours passing without number,
My eyes trace 'round the room. I lay

Dripping sweat and now quite certain
That tonight the final curtain
Drops upon my short life's precious play.

Suddenly a floorboard creak
Announces the bloodsucking freak
Is here to steal my future years away!
A sulf'rous smell now fills the room
Heralding my imm'nent doom!
A fang gleams in the dark and murky gray!

Oh, blood-red eyes and tentacles!
Throbbing, pulsing ventricles!
Mucus-oozing pores and frightful claws!

Worse, in terms of outright scariness,
Are the suckers multifarious
That grab and force you in its mighty jaws!

This disgusting aberration
Of nature needs no motivation
To devour helpless children in their beds.
Relishing despairing moans,
It chews kids up and sucks their bones,
And dissolves inside its mouth their li'l heads!

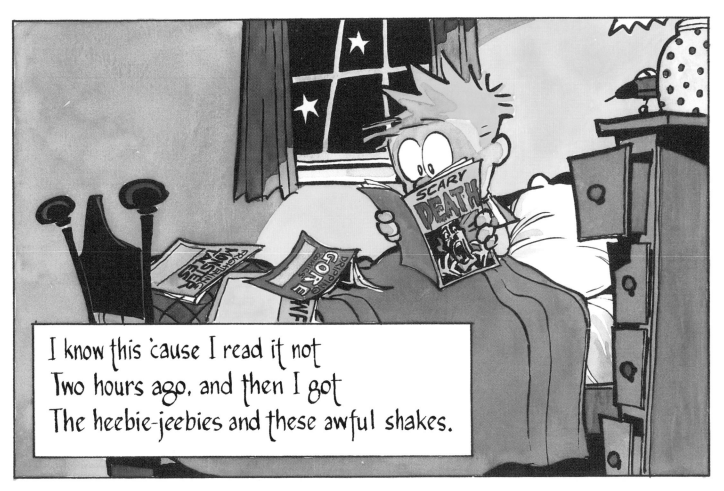

I know this 'cause I read it not
Two hours ago, and then I got
The heebie-jeebies and these awful shakes.

My parents swore upon their honor
That I was safe, and not a goner.
I guess tomorrow they'll see their sad mistakes.

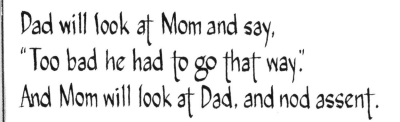

Dad will look at Mom and say,
"Too bad he had to go that way."
And Mom will look at Dad, and nod assent.

Mom will add, "Still, it's fitting,
That as he was this world quitting,
He should leave another mess before he went."

They may not mind at first, I know.
They will miss me later, though,
And perhaps admit that they were wrong.
As memories of me grow dim,
They'll say, "We were too strict with him.
We should have listened to him all along."

As speedily my end approaches,
I bid a final "buenas noches"
To my best friend here in all the world.
Gently snoring, whiskers seeming
To sniff at smells (he must be dreaming),
He lies snuggled in the blankets, curled.

HEY! WAKE UP, YOU STUPID CRETIN!
YOU GONNA SLEEP WHILE I GET EATEN?!
Suddenly the monster knows I'm not alone!

There's an animal in bed with me!
An awful beast he did not see!
The monster never would've come if he had known!

Calvin and Hobbes

by WATTERSON

OUTRAGE! WHY SHOULD I GO TO BED? I'M NOT TIRED! IT'S ONLY 7:30! THIS IS TYRANNY! I'M!

GOOD NIGHT, CALVIN.

WILL YOU CHECK FOR MONSTERS UNDER THE BED?

NO MONSTERS. YOU'RE SAFE.

WHAT ABOUT IN THE DRESSER?

WATTERSON

CALVIN, I'M SURE THERE ARE NO MONSTERS IN YOUR DRESSER. GO TO SLEEP.

GREAT. I'LL BET THAT'S WHERE THEY ALL ARE. THEY'LL COME OUT AND KILL US AS SOON AS WE FALL ASLEEP.

SO WHO'S GOING TO FALL ASLEEP?

WELL, WE'LL JUST HAVE TO GET THE MONSTERS FIRST. YOU IRRITATE THEM WITH THIS HORN, AND I'LL NAIL 'EM WITH MY DART GUN WHEN THEY COME OUT!

GET READY! I HEAR ONE COMING!

HONK HONK HONK HONK HON HOR HONK

WHAT'S ALL THE NOISE?!

AAIEEE!! A MONSTER IN THE HALLWAY!!

DEAR, WILL YOU COME UP HERE A MINUTE?

I THINK I WOUNDED HIM. GIVE ME THE BAT AND I'LL FINISH HIM OFF!

ANY MONSTERS UNDER MY BED TONIGHT?!

NOPE!

NO!

UH-UH.

WELL, THERE'D BETTER **NOT** BE! I'D HATE TO HAVE TO **TORCH** ONE WITH MY FLAME THROWER!

YOU HAVE A FLAME THROWER ??

THEY LIE. I LIE.

MOM, CAN I DRIVE ON THE WAY BACK?

OF COURSE NOT, CALVIN.

CAN I JUST STEER THEN? I PROMISE I WON'T CRASH.

NO, CALVIN.

CAN I WORK THE GAS AND BRAKES WHILE **YOU** STEER?

NO, CALVIN.

YOU NEVER LET ME DO ANYTHING.

HERE WE FIND A THRIVING CITY: BRAND NEW BUILDINGS, A BUSTLING ECONOMY.

A SCENIC THOROUGHFARE WINDS THROUGH THIS HAPPY MUNICIPALITY. HERE, A FARMER DRIVES HIS LIVESTOCK TO MARKET.

TRAGICALLY, THIS SERENE METROPOLIS LIES DIRECTLY BENEATH THE HOOVER DAM...

Calvin and Hobbes by WATTERSON

BAD NEWS, DAD. YOUR POLLS ARE WAY DOWN.

MY POLLS?

YOU RATE ESPECIALLY LOW AMONG TIGERS AND SIX-YEAR-OLD WHITE MALES.

IF YOU WANT TO STAY "DAD," I'D SUGGEST YOU ADOPT SOME KEY PLANKS TO YOUR PLATFORM.

SOME SPECIAL INTEREST GROUPS ARE IN FOR A SURPRISE.

OF THOSE POLLED, VIRTUALLY ALL FAVOR INCREASED ALLOWANCES AND THE COMMENCEMENT OF DRIVING LESSONS.

THERE'S A NEW GIRL IN OUR CLASS.

WELL! WHAT'S HER NAME?

WHO KNOWS?

IS SHE NICE?

WHO CARES? NOT ME!

DO YOU *LIKE* HER??

NO!

HERE COMES THAT NEW GIRL.

HEY SUSIE DERKINS, IS THAT YOUR FACE, OR IS A 'POSSUM STUCK IN YOUR COLLAR?

I HOPE YOU SUFFER A DEBILITATING BRAIN ANEURYSM, YOU FREAK!

SHE'S *CUTE*, ISN'T SHE??

GO AWAY.

OH, MARY, YOU LOOK **RAVISHING** IN THAT SKIMPY NEGLIGEE!

KISS KISS

MMM...DARLING, DON'T YOU WISH WE WERE MARRIED?

BUT WE **ARE**! ...OR DID YOU MEAN TO EACH OTHER?

KISS KISS

I'VE GOT TO HAVE YOU! LET'S MURDER OUR SPOUSES!

MURDER?!--YOU SICK ANIMAL! I LOVE IT WHEN YOU TALK THAT WAY! COME HERE!

KISS KISS

SOMETIMES I THINK I LEARN MORE WHEN I STAY HOME FROM SCHOOL.

KISS KISS

MOM, CAN I SET FIRE TO MY BED MATTRESS?

NO, CALVIN.

CAN I RIDE MY TRICYCLE ON THE ROOF?

NO, CALVIN.

THEN CAN I HAVE A COOKIE?

NO, CALVIN.

SHE'S ON TO ME.

NO, MOM! DON'T PUT ME TO BED!

I INSTRUCTED HOBBES TO MESSILY DEVOUR ANYONE WHO BRINGS ME IN BEFORE 9 P.M.!

YOUR STUFFED TIGER IS IN THE WASHING MACHINE.

FINE TIME TO TAKE A **BATH**!

LISTEN, JUST BECAUSE **YOU** NEVER TAKE ONE...

PBT8!

29

WE JOIN OUR HERO MEGAZORKS ABOVE PLANET GLOOB...

SPACEMAN SPIFF, CONQUEROR OF THE COSMOS, IS PURSUED BY THE HIDEOUS SCUM BEINGS OF PLANET Q-13!

SPIFF'S HYPER-FREEM DRIVE MALFUNCTIONS! THE ALIENS CLOSE IN!

SUDDENLY, A SEARING BOLT OF DEADLY FRAP RAY SLICES ACROSS THE BLACKNESS! OUR HERO IS UNFAZED.

ANOTHER BOLT! SPIFF IS HIT!!

PLOOIE!

SPIFF IS GOING DOWN! CAN HE MAKE IT?? IS THIS THE END?!?

AAAAAAH

SPIFF'S ALIVE! HE MADE IT!!

I'M ALIVE! HA HA HA! I KISS THE SWEET GROUND!

MAYBE YOU SHOULD PLAY ON THE SWINGS, CALVIN.

CALVIN, ARE YOU GOING TO TAKE THAT STUFFED TIGER TO SCHOOL AGAIN?

SURE.

DON'T THE KIDS MAKE FUN OF YOU?

TOMMY CHESNUTT DID ONCE, AND NOW NOBODY DOES.

WHY, WHAT HAPPENED TO TOMMY CHESNUTT?

HOBBES ATE HIM!

UGH! HE NEEDED A BATH, TOO...

CALVIN! WHAT'S ALL THIS NOISE?! YOU'RE SUPPOSED TO BE ASLEEP!

MONSTERS UNDER THE BED, DAD! I WAS WHACKING ONE WITH MY BASEBALL BAT!

GOODNESS CALVIN, IT'S JUST YOUR STUFFED TIGER! YOU SHOULD PUT AWAY YOUR TOYS!

SORRY, OL' BUDDY. GOOD THING I MISSED OCCASIONALLY, HUH?

YEAH. LET ME SEE YOUR BAT A MINUTE.

HERE COMES THE SPORTS CAR AT 200 MILES PER HOUR!

HERE COMES A CEMENT TRUCK! LOOK OUT!

AND HERE COMES AN INFLAMMABLE CHEMICAL TRUCK! OH NO!!

THIS OUGHT TO BE GOOD...

31

DIG
DIG

PAT
PAT

CALVIN! WHAT ARE YOU DOING TO OUR YARD ?!?

MAKING SPEED BUMPS.

I WONDER WHERE WE GO WHEN WE DIE.

PITTSBURGH?

YOU MEAN IF WE'RE GOOD OR IF WE'RE BAD?

WE'RE LOST AGAIN.

HA! WE'RE BRAVE EXPLORERS!

THE WORD "LOST" ISN'T EVEN IN OUR VOCABULARY!

HOW ABOUT THE WORD "MOMMY"?

MOMMMYYY !!

HEY! WHERE'S THE STOCKING FOR **HOBBES**?

WHERE'S SANTA GONNA STICK HOBBES' LOOT, IF HOBBES DOESN'T HAVE A STOCKING?!?

OKAY, OKAY... I'LL MAKE HOBBES A STOCKING. DON'T WORRY.

MAKE IT BIG, BUT NOT AS BIG AS MINE.

..."HOBBES' LOOT" ??

DON'T LOOK AT **ME**! I'M *DONE* SHOPPING!

ARE YOU STILL AWAKE?

OF COURSE!

IT'S MIDNIGHT. LET'S GO!

AS SOON AS HE DROPS THE BAG DOWN, YOU GRAB IT, AND I'LL CLOSE THE FLUE!

UH, HOBBES?... I FORGOT TO GET YOU A PRESENT. I DIDN'T EVEN MAKE YOU A CARD...

I'M SORRY, HOBBES. I DIDN'T MEAN TO FORGET.

IT'S OKAY, LITTLE BUDDY. I DIDN'T GET YOU ANYTHING EITHER.

BUT HERE'S A TIGER HUG FOR BEING MY BEST FRIEND.

NOT SO HARD, YOU BIG SISSY. YOU SQUEEZE MY TEARS OUT.

MERRY CHRISTMAS.

IT SAYS HERE THAT BY THE AGE OF SIX ...

.. MOST CHILDREN HAVE SEEN A MILLION MURDERS ON TELEVISION.

I FIND THAT VERY DISTURBING!

IT MEANS I'VE BEEN WATCHING ALL THE WRONG CHANNELS.

I'M NOT EATING THIS GREEN STUFF. YECCHH!

GOOD IDEA, CALVIN. IT'S A PLATE OF TOXIC WASTE THAT WILL TURN YOU INTO A MUTANT IF YOU EAT IT.

RRGHHMPHFFG

MMMM SCRAPE URF GLUNK SMACK URF YUM

THERE HAS **GOT** TO BE A BETTER WAY TO MAKE HIM EAT!

AHHHH.. I CAN FEEL IT WORKING..

DAD, HOW COME YOU LIVE IN THIS HOUSE WITH MOM...

.. INSTEAD OF IN AN APARTMENT WITH SEVERAL SCANTILY CLAD FEMALE ROOMMATES?

BOY! ASK A SIMPLE QUESTION, AND GET ALL YOUR TELEVISION PRIVILEGES REVOKED.

ALL RIGHT, CLASS, WHO WOULD LIKE TO GIVE HIS BOOK REPORT FIRST?

CALVIN, HOW ABOUT YOU?

CALVIN?

CALVIN?

SPACEMAN SPIFF COOLY DRAWS HIS DEATH RAY BLASTER...

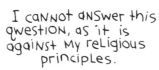

$2 + 7 = \underline{\quad}$

I cannot answer this qwestion, as it is against my religious principles.

IT'S WORTH A SHOT.

HOBBES, WHAT DO YOU THINK HAPPENS TO US WHEN WE DIE?

I THINK WE PLAY SAXOPHONE FOR AN ALL-GIRL CABARET IN NEW ORLEANS.

SO YOU BELIEVE IN HEAVEN?

CALL IT WHAT YOU LIKE.

WE ARE A FIERCE AND DIRTY BAND OF CUTTHROAT PIRATES!

KEEP A SHARP LOOKOUT, MATEY. WE WANT NO SISSY GIRLS ON OUR SHIP!

WE DON'T *LIKE* GIRLS?

OF COURSE NOT, DUMMY! WE'RE A MURDEROUS BUNCH OF *PIRATES*, REMEMBER?!

WHO DO WE SMOOCH THEN?

WHAT DID YOU BRING FOR SHOW AND TELL, SUSIE?

I BROUGHT A LETTER I WROTE TO OUR CONGRESSMAN.

WHAT DID YOU BRING?

A BAG OF DEAD BUGS I COLLECTED FROM OUR WINDOW SILLS.

BEST OF ALL, THIS WAY MOM DIDN'T HAVE TO PACK ME A LUNCH!

WELL, HOBBES, WE DID IT AGAIN. WE'RE SEPARATED FROM THE TROOP AND HOPELESSLY LOST.

FORTUNATELY, OUR MOTTO IS "BE PREPARED."

WITH THIS FULL BACKPACK, WE CAN STAY OUT HERE FOR WEEKS!

JUST SO LONG AS WE DON'T GET HUNGRY.

CALVIN, I DON'T WANT TO BE SPANKED!

WHAT IF IT GOES ON OUR ACADEMIC TRANSCRIPTS? WE'LL BE RUINED!

* SNIFF *

DARN YOU, CALVIN !! YOU'RE GONNA ANSWER TO MY PARENTS IF I CAN'T GET MY MASTER'S DEGREE!

CALVIN AND SUSIE, WOULD YOU COME IN MY OFFICE, PLEASE?

PRINCI

IT WAS ALL HIS FAULT, MR. SPITTLE!

THAT'S A LIE! SHE STARTED IT!

ARE YOU GOING TO SPANK US ??

I'LL NEVER PASS NOTES AGAIN! DON'T SPANK US !!

WAAAHHHH!! I WISH WE WERE DEAD !!

I HATE THIS JOB.

NOW I WANT YOU BOTH TO PAY BETTER ATTENTION IN CLASS, UNDERSTOOD?

YES SIR.

OKAY, YOU MAY RETURN TO YOUR ROOM NOW.

THANK YOU, MR. SPITTLE.

CALVIN? YOU MAY RETURN TO YOUR ROOM.

CALVIN?

THE ZORG DRAWS NEARER. SPIFF SETS HIS BLASTER ON "MEDIUM WELL"...

.. AND WITH THAT REPORT, WE...

CLICK

BEEEOOooooP

CLICK

RATS.

MOM, CAN I TAKE UP THE FLOORBOARDS IN MY ROOM AND MAKE A SECRET PASSAGEWAY?

OF COURSE NOT, CALVIN. DON'T BE RIDICULOUS.

WHY CAN'T I?

BECAUSE YOU'D COME RIGHT THROUGH THE KITCHEN CEILING. I SAID DON'T DO IT.

OKAY, OKAY...

HOW QUIETLY DO YOU THINK WE CAN NAIL THESE BACK IN?

WHAT'S **THIS** DISGUSTING SLIMY BLOB?

TRY IT. YOU'LL LOVE IT.

OH YEAH? WELL WHAT IF I *DON'T* LOVE IT?!?

THEN IT WILL BUILD CHARACTER.

THAT'S MY DAD. ALWAYS LOOKING OUT FOR ME.

47

"McZARGALD'S ... NEXT EXIT... 50 MEGAZORKS.."

"..OVER 75 MILLION EARTHLINGBURGERS SERVED..."

SPACEMAN SPIFF IS GOING DOWN!!!

WE JOIN OUR HERO AS HE STRUGGLES TO LAND HIS DAMAGED SPACECRAFT!

THE ALTITUDE FLAPS REFUSE TO RESPOND, BUT FEARLESS SPIFF IS UNFAZED!

SPIFF CAREENS THROUGH THE ALIEN CANYON! IS THIS *THE END* ??

NO! MOMENTS BEFORE IMPACT, SPIFF EJECTS!

NOW ARE YOU THROUGH CHARGING AROUND THE HOUSE, OR ARE YOU GOING TO FALL DOWN THE STAIRS AGAIN?

OUR HERO REGAINS CONSCIOUSNESS AT THE FEET OF A SARCASTIC ALIEN...

HI, DAD. IT'S ME, CALVIN!

HOW'S WORK GOING? ...UH HUH... PRETTY DAY OUT, ISN'T IT? ... YEP.....

ARE YOU BRINGING ME HOME ANY PRESENTS TONIGHT? ... NO? WELL, JUST THOUGHT I'D ASK...

LISTEN, I SUPPOSE YOU'RE WONDERING WHY I CALLED...

DAD, YOUR POLLS TOOK A BIG DIVE THIS WEEK.

YOUR "OVERALL DAD PERFORMANCE" RATING WAS ESPECIALLY LOW.

SEE? RIGHT ABOUT YESTERDAY YOUR POPULARITY WENT DOWN THE TUBES.

CALVIN, YOU DIDN'T GET DESSERT YESTERDAY BECAUSE YOU FLOODED THE HOUSE!!

I'D SUGGEST A NEW LINE OF WORK, "DAD"..

THE GIANT SLIMY OCTOPUS OOZES ACROSS THE BEACH.

HIS HIDEOUS PRESENCE TERRORIZES THE SLEEPY WATERFRONT COMMUNITY.

WITH A SUCKER-COVERED TENTACLE, HE GRABS AN UNSUSPECTING TOURIST.

A MUFFLED SCREAM LINGERS IN THE SALTY AIR!

DID YOU WANT SOMETHING, CALVIN?

ACK ICK IG

UH-OH, HERE COMES MOE, THE CLASS BULLY!

Okay twinky, let's have that ball.

SURE, MOE. ALL YOURS

NEVER ARGUE WITH A SIX-YEAR-OLD WHO SHAVES.

WATTERSON

Hey! You took my favorite swing!

THAT'S TRUE, MOE. HOW ABOUT THAT?

..uh..

HIS TRAIN OF THOUGHT IS STILL BOARDING AT THE STATION.

WATTERSON

MOE, I WAS WONDERING SOMETHING.

ARE YOUR MALADJUSTED ANTISOCIAL TENDENCIES THE PRODUCT OF YOUR BERSERK PITUITARY GLAND?

WATTERSON

what?

ISN'T HE GREAT, FOLKS? LET'S GIVE HIM A BIG HAND!

"A BUSHEL IS A UNIT OF WEIGHT EQUAL TO FOUR PECKS."

WHAT'S A PECK?

A QUICK SMOOCH.

YOU KNOW, I DON'T UNDERSTAND MATH AT ALL.

MOM, CAN I HAVE SOME MONEY SO HOBBES AND I CAN GO TO A MOVIE?

WHAT MOVIE?

"THE CUISINART MURDERER OF CENTRAL HIGH."

I REALLY THINK THERE ARE MORE CONSTRUCTIVE WAYS YOU COULD SPEND YOUR AFTERNOON, CALVIN.

WHAT DID SHE SAY?

OH, SHE WENT OFF ON ONE OF HER IRRELEVANT TANGENTS AGAIN.

DO YOU BELIEVE OUR DESTINIES ARE CONTROLLED BY THE STARS?

NO, I THINK WE CAN DO WHATEVER WE WANT WITH OUR LIVES.

NOT TO HEAR MOM AND DAD TELL IT.

WAKE UP, CALVIN. IT'S TIME FOR SCHOOL.

I'M NOT GOING TO SCHOOL ANYMORE.

YOU HAVE TO. IT'S THE LAW.

WHAT ABOUT HOBBES? WHY DOESN'T *HE* HAVE TO GO TO SCHOOL?

HE'S A TIGER. GET UP.

WHAT'S BEING A TIGER GOT TO DO WITH IT?

TIGERS WRECK THE GRADE CURVE.

DO YOU THINK IT'S BETTER TO LIVE IN STUPEFYING SECURITY...

...OR TO TAKE RISKS AND LIVE LIFE ON THE EDGE?

I THINK IT'S BETTER TO ACCEPT DANGER AND LIVE TO THE FULLEST!

I TAKE IT BY YOUR SILENCE THAT YOU AGREE...

I'M MAKING SUSIE DERKINS A VALENTINE.

SHE'S A CUTIE, ALL RIGHT.

SEE, I MADE A BIG RED HEART.

NOW I'M PUTTING LACE AROUND IT.

THAT'S VERY SWEET. I'M SURE SHE'LL LIKE IT.

Susie,
I hate you. Drop dead.
Calvin

I'D LIKE TO GET A VALENTINE BOUQUET FOR A GIRL I KNOW.

WHAT A SWEET LITTLE BOY YOU ARE! COME SEE WHAT WE HAVE.

IS THIS ALL?

DID YOU HAVE SOMETHING SPECIAL IN MIND?

SORT OF. DO YOU HAVE A DUMPSTER OUT BACK I COULD ROOT THROUGH?

CALVIN, YOU BALONEY BRAIN!

YOU SENT ME A HATE-MAIL VALENTINE AND A CRUMMY BUNCH OF DEAD FLOWERS!

SO HERE'S A VALENTINE FOR *YOU*, YOU INSENSITIVE CLOD!!

POW

A VALENTINE AND FLOWERS! HE *LIKES* ME!

SHE NOTICED! SHE *LIKES* ME!

Calvin and Hobbes

by WATTERSON

HEY, CALVIN! ARE WE NEAR A SLAUGHTERHOUSE, OR DID YOU FORGET YOUR DEODORANT?!'

DROP DEAD, SUSIE! YOU'RE SO UGLY, I HEAR YOUR MOM PUTS A BAG OVER YOUR HEAD BEFORE SHE KISSES YOU GOODNIGHT!!

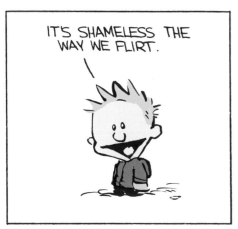

IT'S SHAMELESS THE WAY WE FLIRT.

WHAT'S IT LIKE TO FALL IN LOVE?

WELL... SAY THE OBJECT OF YOUR AFFECTION WALKS BY...

YEAH?

FIRST, YOUR HEART FALLS INTO YOUR STOMACH AND SPLASHES YOUR INNARDS.

ALL THE MOISTURE MAKES YOU SWEAT PROFUSELY.

THIS CONDENSATION SHORTS THE CIRCUITS TO YOUR BRAIN, AND YOU GET ALL WOOZY.

WHEN YOUR BRAIN BURNS OUT ALTOGETHER, YOUR MOUTH DISENGAGES AND YOU BABBLE LIKE A CRETIN UNTIL SHE LEAVES.

THAT'S LOVE?!?

MEDICALLY SPEAKING.

HECK, THAT HAPPENED TO **ME** ONCE, BUT I FIGURED IT WAS **COOTIES!**

WATTERSON

57

Hey, Calvin, it's gonna cost you 50 cents to be my friend today.

AND WHAT IF I DON'T *WANT* TO BE YOUR FRIEND TODAY?

Then the janitor scrapes you off the wall with a spatula.

HECK, WHAT'S A LITTLE EXTORTION AMONG FRIENDS?

I GOT THE NEW ALBUM BY SCRAMBLED DEBUTANTE.

ALL THEIR SONGS GLORIFY DEPRAVED VIOLENCE, MINDLESS SEX, AND THE DELIBERATE ABUSE OF DANGEROUS DRUGS.

YOUR MOM'S GOING TO GO INTO CONNIPTIONS WHEN SHE SEES *THIS* LYING AROUND.

WELL I SURE DIDN'T BUY IT FOR THE MUSIC...

MOM, WILL YOU DRIVE ME INTO TOWN?

WHY SHOULD I *DRIVE* YOU, CALVIN? IT'S A PERFECT DAY OUTSIDE!

WHAT DO YOU THINK PEOPLE HAVE *FEET* FOR?

TO WORK THE GAS PEDAL.

WHEN I GROW UP, I WANT TO BE A RADICAL TERRORIST.

MM HMM..

I'M GOING TO INHALE THIS CAN OF PESTICIDE.

MM HMM..

I'M GOING TO WATCH TV ALL NIGHT.

THAT'S WHAT *YOU* THINK, BUSTER!

YOU CAN NEVER TELL IF THEY'RE LISTENING OR NOT.

WATTERSON

HERE'S A GOOD MOVIE! "VAMPIRE SORORITY BABES"!

IT SAYS YOU HAVE TO BE EIGHTEEN TO GET IN.

HECK, THAT'S NO PROBLEM! LET'S GO!

THIS IS A NEW ONE.

TWO PLEASE. ...I MEAN, ONE.

WATTERSON

I THINK IT'S TIME WE HAD A NEW DAD AROUND HERE. WHEN DOES YOUR TERM OF OFFICE EXPIRE?

SORRY, CALVIN, I WAS APPOINTED DAD FOR LIFE.

FOR LIFE?! WHAT ABOUT A RECALL VOTE? WHAT ABOUT IMPEACHMENT?

THERE ARE NO PROVISIONS FOR EITHER.

DID YOU WRITE THIS CONSTITUTION YOURSELF, OR WHAT?

WELL, YOUR MOM HELPED SOME, TOO.

WATTERSON

You're gonna taste asphalt fifth period, Twinky. Just so you know.

GREAT. I'M DEAD.

FIFTH PERIOD - "STUDIES IN CONTEMPORARY STATE-SPONSORED TERRORISM."

...ALSO KNOWN AS GYM CLASS.

I CAN'T GET A BABY SITTER ANYWHERE! WHAT SHOULD WE DO?

WE WON'T BE GONE LONG. COULDN'T CALVIN BE LEFT FOR A COUPLE HOURS UNSUPERVISED?

HA HA HA HA HA HO HO HO HO HO HEE HE HA HOO HO HAR HA HO H

...SERIOUSLY... WHAT SHOULD WE DO?

HEE HEE

OKAY, CALVIN, WE'LL BE BACK IN A COUPLE OF HOURS.

YOU AND HOBBES JUST WATCH TV AND BE GOOD, OKAY?

DID YOU HEAR THAT? WE GET TO WATCH TV!!

HOORAY!

VIDEORAMA? I'D LIKE TO RENT A VCR AND SOME MOVIES!

ASK IF THEY HAVE "ATTACK OF THE COED CANNIBALS."

WELL, THE HOUSE IS STILL STANDING. CALVIN MUST HAVE GONE TO BED.

HIS LIGHT IS STILL ON. ...CALVIN? ARE YOU AWAKE?

EEP!

DID YOU WATCH A SCARY MOVIE ?!?

NO. DON'T COME IN. THE RUG IS RIGGED TOO.

WHAP!

SMASH

TINKLE
DING
SHATTER
CLINK

WOW. FIRST TRY!

DOWNTOWN TOKYO!

AARRGHHGH!

GODZILLA.

Calvin and Hobbes
by WATTERSON

HOW CAN I GET SOME MONEY?

...SHORT OF EARNING IT, I MEAN...

I WANT A GRENADE LAUNCHER, MOM. WHEN'S CHRISTMAS?

NOT FOR A LONG TIME.

WHEN'S MY BIRTHDAY?

NOT FOR A LONG TIME.

WHEN'S MY ALLOWANCE?

YOU SPENT IT ALREADY.

DO I HAVE ANY STOCKS I CAN CASH? WAR BONDS??

CALVIN, I'M TRYING TO WORK!

CAN I BORROW SOME SOAP?

YES, YOU CAN BORROW SOME SOAP. HAVE ALL THE SOAP YOU WANT.

4 Sale CHEEP!

BOY, IS IT COLD!

YOU SHOULD GET A GOOD FUR COAT LIKE MINE.

WOOF! WHAT DID YOU EAT FOR BREAKFAST? CEMENT?

LOOK, WAS THIS *MY* IDEA?

OH NO, I LOST MY QUARTER!

WHERE DID YOU LOSE IT?

IT'S SOMEWHERE IN THIS FIELD.

WE'LL NEVER FIND IT. YOU'LL HAVE TO WAIT TILL THE SNOW MELTS.

TILL THE SNOW MELTS? IT'S 25 CENTS!!

ZZZZZZZ

WANNA SEE SOMETHING WEIRD?

WATCH. YOU PUT BREAD IN THIS SLOT AND PUSH DOWN THIS LEVER...

THEN IN A FEW MINUTES, TOAST POPS UP!

DING.

WOW. WHERE DOES THE BREAD GO?

BEATS ME. ISN'T THAT WEIRD?

HOW ARE YOU TODAY?

FINE.

I WANT THE TOP OF MY HEAD SHAVED, AND THE SIDES DYED PINK AND CUT IN HORIZONTAL STRIPES, OK?

MA'AM?

GIVE HIM THE USUAL, PETE.

WELL I GUESS THIS GUY KNOWS WHICH SIDE *HIS* BREAD IS BUTTERED ON!

THERE, HOW'S THAT LOOK?

THAT'S GREAT. PERFECT.

WITHOUT QUESTION, THIS IS THE FINEST HAIRCUT I HAVE EVER RECEIVED.

NEVER CRITICIZE A GUY WITH A RAZOR...

TOO BAD THE WORLD WILL BE ENDING SOON.

BEG YOUR PARDON?

HALLEY'S COMET. COMETS ARE HARBINGERS OF DOOM.

NO, THEY AREN'T. THAT'S JUST SUPERSTITION.

REALLY??

GUESS I'D BETTER WRITE THAT BOOK REPORT.

DO YOU LOVE ME, DAD?

OF COURSE I DO, CALVIN.

WOULD YOU STILL LOVE ME IF I DID SOMETHING BAD?

WELL OF COURSE ... I ... WOULD...

I MEAN SOMETHING REALLY *REALLY*..

CALVIN, WHAT DID YOU DO?!

WELL, DAD, YOUR POLLS ARE REAL HIGH THIS WEEK.

I'M GLAD TO HEAR THAT.

YEP, THOSE POLLED THINK YOU'RE DOING A FINE JOB AS DAD.

IN FACT, WITH A LITTLE PUSH TODAY, YOUR POLITICAL STOCK COULD REACH A RECORD HIGH.

NICE TRY. GO HELP YOUR MOM WITH THE DISHES.

OOH DAD! SUICIDE! OOH! OOH!

HERE COMES MOE, THE CLASS BULLY.

HE'S NOT SMART, BUT HE'S STREETWISE.

THAT MEANS HE KNOWS WHAT STREET HE LIVES ON.

CAN I BE EXCUSED?

NOT UNTIL YOU FINISH YOUR SALMON.

BLAUGHHH!

CAN I EAT IT UPSTAIRS WHILE I DO MY HOMEWORK?

WELL, I SUPPOSE.

I BROUGHT YOU YOUR FAVORITE! HOW'S IT COMING?

WELL, I COULDN'T FIGURE OUT THIS SUBTRACTION PROBLEM, SO I PUT "ATLANTA, GEORGIA"...

HEY, SUSIE, WANNA SEE A MAGIC TRICK?

FIRST, I'LL NEED AN ORDINARY QUARTER...

NOW I'LL DISAPPEAR! HA HA HA!

!

HEY! DIDN'T I SAY IT WAS A TRICK??

LOOK! A DECODER RING!

WOW! WE CAN SEND EACH OTHER SECRET MESSAGES IN CODE!

HA HA! NOW MOM AND DAD WON'T BE ABLE TO UNDERSTAND US AT ALL!

... NOT THAT THEY DO ANYWAY...

RISE AND SHINE, CALVIN!

MFGPBTHBBPT

THE EARLY BIRD GETS THE WORM!

BIG INCENTIVE.

I'VE DECIDED WE SHOULD BE "COOLER" THAN WE ARE.

WE'RE NOT COOL?

SURE WE'RE COOL. BUT WE'RE NOT AS COOL AS WE **COULD** BE.

COOL PEOPLE WEAR DARK GLASSES!

IT'S COOL TO BUMP INTO THINGS?

YOU DON'T MOVE, YOU JUST HANG AROUND.

HEY, DAD, WILL YOU BUY ME A FLAME THROWER?

OF COURSE NOT. DON'T BE SILLY.

EVEN IF I DIDN'T USE IT IN THE HOUSE?

I TOLD YOU I'M NOT SICK! WHAT'S THAT? WILL IT HURT?

IT'S A TONGUE DEPRESSOR. IT WON'T HURT AT ALL.

WHAT'S *THAT*? WILL IT HURT?

IT'S A STETHOSCOPE. IT WON'T HURT AT ALL.

WHAT'S *THAT*? WILL IT HURT?

IT'S A CATTLE PROD. IT HURTS A LITTLE LESS THAN A BRANDING IRON.

LITTLE KIDS HAVE NO SENSE OF HUMOR.

HEY, DOC, WHY ARE YOU RUBBING MY ARM WITH COTTON? ARE YOU GOING TO PUT A LEECH THERE?

ARE YOU GOING TO BLEED ME? YOU'RE NOT GOING TO AMPUTATE, ARE YOU? **ARE** YOU??

WHAT'S THAT? IS THAT A SHOT? ARE YOU GOING TO... **AAUGHH! IT WENT CLEAR THROUGH MY ARM!!** OW OW OW OW!!!

I'M DYING! I HOPE YOU'VE PAID YOUR MALPRACTICE INSURANCE, YOU QUACK!! **WHERE'S MY MOM??!**

"SAFARI AL" HACKS HIS WAY THROUGH THE JUNGLE!

SUDDENLY, A GIANT GORILLA RIPS THROUGH THE FOLIAGE!

CLEAN YOUR ROOM.

WHAT?

YOU HEARD ME. IT'S A JUNGLE IN HERE!

SOMEWHERE IN COMMUNIST RUSSIA I'LL BET THERE'S A LITTLE BOY WHO HAS NEVER KNOWN ANYTHING BUT **CENSORSHIP** AND **OPPRESSION**.

BUT MAYBE HE'S HEARD ABOUT **AMERICA**, AND HE DREAMS OF LIVING IN THIS LAND OF **FREEDOM** AND OPPORTUNITY!

SOMEDAY, I'D LIKE TO MEET THAT LITTLE BOY...

...AND TELL HIM THE AWFUL **TRUTH** ABOUT THIS PLACE!!

CALVIN, BE QUIET AND EAT THE STUPID LIMA BEANS.

WHENEVER I TAKE MY BATH...

...I ALWAYS PUT MY DUCKY IN FIRST.

FOR COMPANIONSHIP?

TO TEST FOR SHARKS.

MY SECRET ANCIENT TREASURE MAP SAYS TO DIG HERE!

LOOK! A WALLET FULL OF MONEY! RIGHT WHERE YOU SAID!

IT'S DAD'S. I BURIED IT HERE LAST WEEK.

SPACEMAN SPIFF, BOLD INTERPLANETARY EXPLORER, SPIES A ZARG!

SPIFF CALIBRATES HIS BLASTER. READY...AIM...

CALVIN, IF YOU SHOOT THAT PAPER CLIP AT ME, I'LL GET YOUR BOTTOM HAULED TO THE PRINCIPAL'S OFFICE SO FAST YOU'LL THINK YOU WERE IN A **TIME WARP**!!

CONFOUND IT. THE BLASTER JAMMED.

IT LOOKS LIKE HOBBES BURST A SEAM HERE. I'LL GET MY SEWING KIT.

IT'S JUST A LITTLE CUT. I DON'T NEED AN OPERATION. THIS IS UNNECESSARY SURGERY!

IT'S NOT SURGERY. YOU'RE JUST GETTING A COUPLE STITCHES! WHAT'S THE BIG DEAL?

YOUR MOM NEVER USES ANY ANESTHETIC.

WHAT A PECULIAR DREAM I HAD LAST NIGHT!

I DREAMED I WAS IN A BIG FIGHT WITH A FEROCIOUS WEASEL!

WHAT DO YOU SUPPOSE IT MEANS?

IT MEANS YOU'RE SLEEPING ON THE FLOOR TONIGHT, YOU NINCOMPOOP!

Calvin and Hobbes by WATTERSON

WHY SURE.

HEY DAD, REMEMBER OUR CAR?

WAIT A MINUTE. WHAT DO YOU MEAN, "REMEMBER"?

HOBBES, I HAVE A CONJECTURAL MORAL QUESTION. MAYBE YOU CAN HELP.

SURE.

SUPPOSE I DID SOMETHING BAD. SHOULD I TELL DAD?

HOW BAD ARE WE SUPPOSING?

WELL, HYPOTHETICALLY, LET'S SAY PRETTY BAD. LIKE TO HIS CAR, HYPOTHETICALLY.

HOW BAD, HYPOTHETICALLY, TO HIS CAR?

WELL, LET'S PRETEND IT WAS REAL BAD.

SHOULD WE PRETEND IT COULD BE FIXED?

IF WE IMAGINED HE COULD FIND THE CAR, WE COULD PRETEND IT MIGHT BE FIXED.

I SEE.

YOU CAN KEEP THE BOOK. I'LL CALL THE BUS STATION.

"¿QUE PASA, SEÑORITA? ¡I AM EL FUGITIVO!"

WHY CAN'T I STAY UP LATE? YOU GUYS CAN!

IT'S NOT FAIR!

THE *WORLD* ISN'T FAIR, CALVIN.

I KNOW, BUT WHY ISN'T IT EVER UNFAIR IN MY FAVOR?

THE VALIANT SPACEMAN SPIFF IS BEING PURSUED BY A DISGUSTING SCUM BEING!

SPIFF SPOTS HIS HOVERING SPACESHIP AND BOLTS FOR THE LADDER!

BUT HE'S TOO LATE! THE AWFUL SCUM BEING IS UPON HIM! IT'S ALL OVER!

IT'S ALL OVER!!

I TOLD YOU **THREE TIMES** RECESS WAS OVER! NOW GET INSIDE!

AS DICTATOR, I HAVE THE SOLE VOICE IN GOVERNMENT!

I WILL NOT TOLERATE DISSENT!

I ALONE SHALL DECIDE THE GOOD! I ALONE SHALL...

TIME FOR BED, CALVIN.

COULDN'T WE VOTE ON THIS?

I CAN'T GET THIS MODEL AIRPLANE TO LOOK RIGHT.

THESE DIRECTIONS ARE IMPOSSIBLE!

RRRRRGGGHHHHH

WHAM WHAM WHAM

HIT BY ANTI-AIRCRAFT GUNS.

YOUR PLANES DO SEEM TO RUN INTO THOSE, DON'T THEY?

TOMMY TOLD A FUNNY STORY AT SCHOOL TODAY. I ALMOST DIED!

TELL IT TO ME.

WELL, ACTUALLY THE STORY ITSELF WASN'T SO FUNNY...

...IT WAS THE *WAY* HE TOLD IT.

HOW DID HE TELL IT?

HE WAS DRINKING MILK AND WHEN HE LAUGHED, IT CAME UP HIS NOSE!

You've got two periods to live, Twinky.

Then it's gym class, and I turn you into hamburger casserole!

I HATE GYM CLASS.

COACH THINKS VIOLENCE IS AEROBIC.

WHERE'S MY JACKET?

I'VE LOOKED EVERYWHERE! UNDER THE BED, OVER MY CHAIR...

...ON THE STAIRS, ON THE HALL FLOOR, IN THE KITCHEN... IT'S JUST NOT ANYWHERE!

OH, *HERE* IT IS! WHO PUT IT IN THE STUPID CLOSET?!?

WATTERSON

HOCUS-POCUS, ABRACADABRA!

I COMMAND MY HOMEWORK TO DO ITSELF! **HOMEWORK, BE DONE!**

WATTERSON

FLIP FLIP FLIP

RATS.

DO YOU EVER THINK ABOUT THE END OF THE WORLD AS WE KNOW IT?

YOU MEAN A NUCLEAR WAR?

WATTERSON

I THINK MOM WAS REFERRING TO IF SHE EVER CATCHES ME LETTING THE AIR OUT OF THE CAR TIRES AGAIN.

86

FEARLESS SPACEMAN SPIFF CLOSES IN ON THE FLEEING ZARGONS!

ONCE AGAIN OUR HERO IS ABOUT TO TEACH VICIOUS ALIEN SCUM THAT VIRTUE IS ITS OWN REWARD! HE LOCKS ONTO TARGET!

PSST, CALVIN! WHAT WAS THE CAPITAL OF POLAND UNTIL 1600?

KRAKOW.

THANKS.

KRAKOW! KRAKOW! TWO DIRECT HITS!

THE TYRANNOSAURUS LUMBERS ACROSS THE PREHISTORIC VALLEY...

THE TERRIFYING LIZARD IS THREE STORIES TALL AND HIS MOUTH IS FILLED WITH SIX-INCH CHISELS OF DEATH!

WITH A FEW MIGHTY STEPS, THE DINOSAUR IS UPON A TRIBE OF FLEEING CAVEMEN. HE DEVOURS THEM ONE BY ONE!

AARRGH! AAIEEE! AAUGHH!

CALVIN, EAT YOUR POPCORN QUIETLY!

WHAT DOES THIS WORD MEAN?

WHICH ONE?

THAT LONG ONE.

I DON'T KNOW.

YOU DO TOO!! ALL RIGHT! WHERE'S A DICTIONARY??

88

CAN I WATCH THE MOVIE "KILLER PROM QUEEN" ON TV?

NO.

DO I HAVE TO EAT THIS SLIMY ASPARAGUS?

YES.

CAN I STAY UP TILL MIDNIGHT?

NO.

THERE'S AN INVERSE RELATIONSHIP BETWEEN HOW GOOD SOMETHING IS FOR YOU, AND HOW MUCH FUN IT IS.

LET'S SEE WHAT HAPPENS IF YOU COOK POPCORN WITHOUT A LID.

POW

KAPWING
POW BANG
ZANG BOING

HECK, THAT'S MORE FUN THAN EXPLODING A POTATO IN THE MICROWAVE!

LET'S DO SOME MORE!

C'MON, CALVIN. WE'RE GOING TO THE STORE.

CAN HOBBES COME?

NO, JUST LEAVE HIM HERE.

BUT I WANT HIM TO COME WITH US!!

IF YOU CAN'T WIN BY REASON, GO FOR VOLUME.

WHACK!

WOW! ANOTHER HOLE IN ONE!

WOW! THREE NEW MAGAZINES FOR ME TODAY.

YESTERDAY I GOT FIVE. I LOVE GETTING ALL THIS MAIL.

HOW COME YOU RECEIVE ALL THESE MAGAZINES?

I WENT TO THE LIBRARY AND FILLED OUT ALL THE SUBSCRIPTION CARDS THAT SAID "BILL ME LATER!"

I LOVE SATURDAY MORNING CARTOONS.

WHAT CLASSIC HUMOR!

THIS IS WHAT ENTERTAINMENT IS ALL ABOUT.

... IDIOTS, EXPLOSIVES, AND FALLING ANVILS.

CALVIN, THE HUMAN INSECT, WALKS ACROSS THE DINNER TABLE.

WITH PROPORTIONAL INSECT STRENGTH, HE PLACES A GIANT PEA ON THE EDGE OF A SPOON.

HE THEN CLIMBS TO THE TOP OF THE OTHER END...

...AND WITH A TINY JUMP...

CALVIN, STOP THAT!

IN HIS MINUSCULE SIZE, IT TAKES CALVIN, THE HUMAN INSECT, TEN MINUTES TO WALK ACROSS A BOOK'S PAGE!

AT THE OTHER END, HE SLOWLY LIFTS THE GIGANTIC SHEET!

THEN IT'S ANOTHER TEN-MINUTE JOURNEY BACK, AS HE TURNS IT OVER!

GEE, THE KID'S BEEN QUIET FOR ALMOST TWENTY MINUTES.

HE'S DOING HIS HOMEWORK.

HERE'S A MOVIE WE SHOULD WATCH.

WHO'S IN IT?

IT SAYS, "JAPANESE CAST."

"TWO BIG RUBBERY MONSTERS SLUG IT OUT OVER MAJOR METROPOLITAN CENTERS IN A BATTLE FOR WORLD SUPREMACY."

DOESN'T THAT SOUND GREAT?

AND PEOPLE SAY THAT FOREIGN FILM IS INACCESSIBLE.

OH, ROSALYN, YOU'RE HERE! GOOD, COME IN!

WE REALLY APPRECIATE YOUR COMING ON SUCH SHORT NOTICE. WE'VE HAD A TERRIBLE TIME GETTING A BABY SITTER FOR TONIGHT.

HA HA, MAYBE LITTLE CALVIN HERE HAS GOTTEN HIMSELF A REPUTATION.

HA HA. YOU HAVE THE HALF UP FRONT?

YES, LET ME GET MY PURSE...

HI, BABY DOLL, IT'S ME. YEAH, I'M BABY SITTING THE KID DOWN THE STREET.

YEAH, THAT'S RIGHT, THE LITTLE MONSTER. ...HMM?... WELL SO FAR, NO PROBLEM.

HE HASN'T BEEN ANY TROUBLE. YOU JUST HAVE TO SHOW THESE KIDS WHO'S THE BOSS...MM HMM..

HOW MUCH LONGER TILL SHE LETS US OUT OF THE GARAGE?

SHE SAID 8 O'CLOCK, AND IT'S ALMOST 6:30 NOW...

THANKS AGAIN FOR BABY SITTING, ROSALYN.

CALVIN WAS NO TROUBLE AT ALL.

THAT'S GOOD. I'LL GET THE CAR AND DRIVE YOU HOME.

THERE YOU GO. GOOD NIGHT.

THANK YOU. GOOD NIGHT.

IS SHE GONE?

WHAT A GREAT NIGHT TO CAMP OUT!

WHERE'S OUR TENT? I THOUGHT THE SCOUTMASTER SAID TO SET THEM UP.

UH OH.

WHEN HE SAID TO PITCH THE TENT, I THREW IT AWAY.

THE BEST PART ABOUT THESE HIKES IS GETTING TO SEE SO MUCH WILDLIFE.

LOOK! A TIGER!

A TIGER?!

DON'T **DO** THAT!

WE'RE SEPARATED FROM THE TROOP AND HOPELESSLY LOST!

LEFT ALONE IN THE UNCOMPROMISING WILD TO SURVIVE BY OUR WITS UNAIDED!

HEY, DUMMY! THE SCOUTMASTER SAYS TO GRAB YOUR STUPID STUFFED TIGER AND GET YOUR REAR IN GEAR!

WE'LL TRY TO LOSE 'EM AGAIN OVER THE NEXT HILL.

GRAB THE HOTDOGS AND COME ON!

THE TROOP'S COOKING DINNER OVER THE FIRE.

OH THAT'S JUST GREAT.

HERE WE'VE BEEN LUGGING THIS DUMB MICROWAVE AROUND FOR NOTHING.

BOP

SPIKE!

OH OH, WE'D BETTER LEAVE!

IT LOOKS LIKE SOME BIG PEOPLE WANT TO PLAY TENNIS.

THE CROCODILE FLOATS TO THE TOP OF THE MURKY AMAZON...

COMPLETELY MOTIONLESS, HE APPEARS TO BE ONLY A HARMLESS LOG.

A HIPPOPOTAMUS APPROACHES AND ENSURES ITS INSTANT DEATH!

CALVIN, WHAT ARE YOU DOING? ARE YOU ALL RIGHT?

CLOSER... CLOSER...

MOM! MOM! A BIG DOG KNOCKED ME DOWN AND HE STOLE HOBBES!

I TRIED TO CATCH HIM, BUT I COULDN'T, AND NOW I'VE LOST MY BEST FRIEND!

WELL CALVIN, IF YOU WOULDN'T DRAG THAT TIGER EVERYWHERE, THINGS LIKE THIS WOULDN'T HAPPEN.

THERE'S NO PROBLEM SO AWFUL THAT YOU CAN'T ADD SOME GUILT TO IT AND MAKE IT EVEN WORSE!

I CAN'T SLEEP AT ALL. POOR HOBBES! I WONDER WHERE HE IS. I HOPE HE'S OK.

SNIFF.. WHAT DID I EVER DO TO DESERVE THIS?

WHATEVER IT WAS, I'M *SORRY* ALREADY!

LOST: MY TIGER, "HOBBES"

MAYBE YOU SHOULD DESCRIBE HIM.

ON THE QUIET SIDE. SOMEWHAT PECULIAR. A GOOD COMPANION, IN A WEIRD SORT OF WAY.

I MEAN, WHAT DOES HE LOOK LIKE?

OH.

WELL LOOK, SOMEBODY LEFT A STUFFED TIGER OUT IN THE FIELD. HOW STRANGE.

LOOKS LIKE A DOG'S BEEN CHEWING ON YOU, FELLA.

WELL, NOTHING A LITTLE TEA PARTY WITH SOME OTHER STUFFED ANIMALS WOULDN'T HELP. C'MON.

HOBBES! HOBBES! WHERE ARE YOU?!?

HELLO, CALVIN. WOULD YOU LIKE TO JOIN MY TEA PARTY?

HECK NO. I'M TRYING TO FIND MY BEST FRIEND, WHO'S BEEN KIDNAPPED BY A DOG. LEAVE ME ALONE.

WELL I THINK MR. CALVIN IS VERY RUDE, DON'T YOU, MR. TIGER? YES, I THINK SO TOO. MORE TEA, ANYONE?

HEY, I SHOULD TELL SUSIE TO KEEP HER EYES OPEN FOR HOBBES.

SUSIE, I... *HOBBES!*

YOU FOUND HOBBES! THANK YOU THANK YOU THANKYOUTHANKYOUTHANKY OUTHANKYOUTHANKYOUTHA

WELL! WASN'T MR. CALVIN A GENTLEMAN! I DO HOPE... *HEY!* WHO TOOK ALL THE COOKIES?!?

calvin and Hobbes by WATTERSON

WHAT'S THAT SMELL?

EITHER MOM'S COOKING DINNER, OR SOMEBODY GOT SICK IN THE FURNACE DUCT.

BOY, DOES IT **STINK** IN HERE! WHAT ARE YOU COOKING FOR DINNER?!

WHATEVER IT IS, I'M NOT EATING IT.

I'M STEWING SOME MONKEY HEADS.

MONKEY HEADS?

THEY'LL BE SOGGY ENOUGH TO EAT IN ABOUT TWENTY MINUTES.

WATTERSON

REALLY?? WE'RE HAVING MONKEY HEADS? WE ARE NOT. ...ARE THOSE REALLY MONKEY HEADS?

I'VE NEVER HAD MONKEY HEADS BEFORE! I WONDER WHAT THEY'RE LIKE.

WOW! MONKEY HEADS!

MM...KINDA SQUISHY. OOH LOOK, IS THAT A NOSE? WHAT'S THIS? BRAINS? I DIDN'T THINK THEY'D BE SO RUBBERY...

WHAT? I THOUGHT THESE WERE STUFFED PEPPERS. HONEY, WHAT THE HECK **IS** THIS?? WHATEVER IT IS, I'M NOT EATING IT!

Panel 1: SUSIE, WANNA HEAR A SECRET?

SURE.

Panel 2: I THINK THE PRINCIPAL IS A SPACE ALIEN SPY.

Panel 3: HE'S TRYING TO CORRUPT OUR YOUNG INNOCENT MINDS SO WE'LL BE UNABLE TO RESIST WHEN HIS PEOPLE INVADE EARTH!

Panel 4: PROMISE NOT TO TELL ANYONE?

DON'T WORRY.

Panel 5: HOBBES, WHAT SHOULD I DO WHEN MOE COMES TO BEAT ME UP IN GYM CLASS?

Panel 6: WELL, YOU CAN ALWAYS DO WHAT WE TIGERS DO WHEN A RHINO CHARGES.

Panel 7: WHAT'S THAT?

WE SCRAMBLE LIKE MANIACS FOR THE NEAREST TREE.

Panel 8: THAT'S YOUR ADVICE?? TO SIT IN A TREE ALL DAY?!?

IT DOESN'T IMPRESS THE GIRLS, OF COURSE, BUT THERE'S NO SENSE IMPRESSING THEM AND THEN GETTING KILLED, MY DAD USED TO SAY...

Panel 9: HOBBES, I NEED YOUR HELP. THAT BULLY MOE KEEPS PUSHING ME AROUND.

Panel 10: ...SO I WANT YOU TO COME TO SCHOOL AND EAT HIM, OK?

Panel 11: EAT HIM?

SURE! TIGERS EAT PEOPLE ALL THE TIME!

Panel 12: WHAT IF THE CAFETERIA LADIES WON'T LET ME USE THE OVEN?

IT'S TOO EARLY TO BE IN BED. IT'S HARDLY EVEN DARK OUT. WHY DO I HAVE TO BE IN BED? IT'S RIDICULOUS.

I'M NOT EVEN TIRED! I DON'T NEED TO BE IN BED! THIS IS AN OUTRAGE!

IT'S THE STUPIDEST THING I CAN IMAGINE! I THINK MOM AND DAD ARE JUST TRYING TO GET RID OF ME. I CAN'T SLEEP AT ALL. CAN YOU SLEEP, HOBBES?

NO!

OK, MOM, HOBBES AND I HAVE FORMED A LOBBY. WE WANT MORE PRIVILEGES!

MORE PRIVILEGES? LIKE WHAT? YOU'VE GOT IT MADE!

NO RESPONSIBILITIES, NO CARES, NO WORRIES! WHAT MORE COULD YOU POSSIBLY WANT?

WHY DIDN'T YOU TELL HER ABOUT THE CREDIT CARDS IN OUR NAMES?

YOU HEARD HER. SHE'S IN ONE OF HER MOODS.

I LOVE SATURDAYS!

EVERY SATURDAY I GET UP AT SIX AND EAT THREE BOWLS OF CRUNCHY SUGAR BOMBS.

THEN I WATCH CARTOONS TILL NOON, AND I'M INCOHERENT AND HYPERACTIVE THE REST OF THE DAY.

DOES IT WORK?

NO BROTHERS OR SISTERS **SO** FAR!

IN THE COMMERCIALS, THIS COLA GREATLY INCREASES ONE'S SEX APPEAL.

GLIK
GLIK
GLICK
GLICK

BUR-UR-URPP!!

EVIDENTLY A LITTLE LICENSE ON MADISON AVENUE'S PART.

PHOO! RIGHT UP MY NOSE.

IT'S AN OUTRAGE THAT SIX-YEAR-OLDS CAN'T VOTE!

HERE I AM, A U.S. CITIZEN, WITH NO VOICE IN OUR REPRESENTATIVE GOVERNMENT!

YOU'RE CONCERNED ABOUT THE DIRECTION THE COUNTRY IS HEADED?

NO, I JUST WANT A BIGGER PIECE OF THE PIE.

POOF
POOF
POOF

POW!

GOOD HEAVENS, I THINK I BLEW MY FACE INSIDE OUT!

THE WATER'S TOO COLD!

NOW IT'S TOO HOT.

NOW IT'S TOO COLD.

NOW IT'S TOO DEEP.

THE FEARSOME SHARK SENSES DISTRESS IN THE WAVES ABOVE HIM!

HE CIRCLES UP, CLOSER AND CLOSER TO THE TERRIFIED VICTIM!

HEY! YAHH! SNAP THRASH SNAP!

YOU KNOW, FOR SOMEONE WHO HATES BATHS AS MUCH AS YOU DO, YOU'RE NOT MAKING THIS GO ANY FASTER!

ANOTHER GRUESOME KILL...

HERE, CALVIN, I'LL SHOW YOU A MAGIC TRICK.

SEE? I PULLED A DIME FROM YOUR EAR! PRETTY GOOD, HUH?

ANYTHING YET?

J-JUST A B-B-BLOODY N-NOSE.

Calvin and Hobbes
by WATTERSON

WE SHOULD MAKE DAD A FATHER'S DAY CARD.

OKAY, I'LL DRAW A PICTURE OF HIM ON IT.

HMM... MAKE HIS MOUTH BIGGER. HE USUALLY LOOKS ANGRIER THAN THAT.

GOOD MORNING, DAD! HAPPY FATHER'S DAY!

MMF. GOOMRG.

IN APPRECIATION OF YOUR SERVICE AS DAD, TODAY I AM LIVING ACCORDING TO THE PRINCIPLES OF YOUR FATHERLY WISDOM.

CALVIN, WHAT TIME IS...

FIVE IN THE MORNING?!

YES, "EARLY TO BED, EARLY TO RISE," YOU ALWAYS SAY...

I WAS GOING TO BUY YOU A NICE PRESENT, BUT "A PENNY SAVED IS A PENNY EARNED," AS YOU SAY...

..SO I'M NOW EARNING 6% ON THE MONEY I DIDN'T SPEND.

YES, DAD, THANKS TO YOU, I'M A HAPPIER, BETTER PERSON.

GOOD WORK, SOCRATES.

I KNEW WE'D MADE A MISTAKE THE MINUTE I SAW THAT LITTLE BOLOGNA LOAF IN THE HOSPITAL BASSINET.

I'VE NEVER BEEN THIS HIGH IN A TREE BEFORE.

ME EITHER. YOU CAN SEE FOR MILES FROM UP HERE.

I'LL SAY! I'M GLAD WE'RE UP HERE.

THAT WAS QUITE A CRASH, WASN'T IT?

THE RAIN STOPPED!

THIS IS THE BEST TIME TO GO WORMUCKING. LET'S GO!

WHAT'S THAT?

IT'S WHEN YOU WALK ON THE PAVEMENT AND MUCK ALL THE WORMS.

CALVIN, QUIT CHARGING AROUND THE HOUSE!!

SMASH!
BINK
BONK
BOOM

WHAT DID I JUST TELL YOU?!?

BEATS ME. WEREN'T YOU LISTENING EITHER?

WHEN ARE WE GOING TO GET TO OUR VACATION SITE? I WANNA *BE* THERE!

CALVIN, IT'S AN EIGHT-HOUR DRIVE. WE'RE NOT EVEN OUT OF OUR STATE YET. IT'S GOING TO BE A WHILE. RELAX.

HOW MUCH LONGER *NOW*?

I TOLD YOU WE SHOULD HAVE FLOWN.

THERE'S A RESTAURANT COMING UP. WANT TO STOP?

ONLY IF THEY HAVE HAMBURGERS.

HAMBURGERS? THAT'S ALL WE'VE EATEN THIS WHOLE STUPID TRIP! HAMBURGERS, HAMBURGERS, HAMBURGERS!

I'M SICK OF HAMBURGERS! WE'RE EATING SOMETHING ELSE FOR ONCE!

TEN MILLION BOTTLES OF BEER ON THE WALL, TEN MILLION BOTTLES OF BEER...

OK! OK! HERE'S A HAMBURGER JOINT! *ARE YOU HAPPY?!*

I HAVE TO GO TO THE BATHROOM.

CALVIN, WE JUST PULLED OUT OF THE RESTAURANT. CAN'T YOU WAIT? THINK OF SOMETHING ELSE.

ALL I CAN THINK OF IS NIAGARA FALLS, AND THE HOOVER DAM, AND NOAH'S ARK, AND...

OOH BOY, NOW *I* HAVE TO GO!

NEXT YEAR I SWEAR I'LL JUST TAKE A VACATION BY MYSELF.

THAT TRIP WAS EXCRUCIATING. THANK GOODNESS WE'RE HERE.

EIGHT HOURS CRAMMED IN A CAR WITH A HYPERACTIVE SIX-YEAR-OLD! WHAT AN ORDEAL!

WELL, NOW CALVIN CAN RUN AND SCREAM ALL HE LIKES. AHH, WHAT A GREAT LITTLE PLACE.

I'M BORED. WHEN ARE WE LEAVING?

YOU'RE BORED? WOULD YOU LIKE ME TO SHOW YOU HOW AN ANCHOR WORKS?

AHH! ANOTHER GLORIOUS SUNRISE, AND NOT A SOUL AROUND!

THIS IS THE LIFE! A BRISK SWIM AT DAWN, A MORNING OUT IN A BOAT...

...AND BY 9 A.M., I'M BACK WITH FRESHLY CAUGHT FISH FOR BREAKFAST! THE DAY'S HARDLY BEGUN! WHAT A VACATION!

UGH...I'VE SEEN CHEERIER FACES AT THE OFFICE!

YOU EAT YOUR DEAD ANIMALS. ALL I WANT IS SOME COFFEE.

WHY ISN'T THERE ANY TV UP HERE? I HATE THIS PLACE.

DAD, LOOK! I CAUGHT A FISH!

HEY, THAT'S A BIG ONE. I'LL SHOW YOU HOW TO CLEAN IT, AND WE'LL HAVE IT FOR DINNER.

"CLEAN IT"?

CUT OFF ITS HEAD AND GUT IT.

MMM! PASS ME ANOTHER OF THESE GREAT CHEESE SANDWICHES! HA HA, NO BONES IN THESE, RIGHT?

C'MON, CALVIN! I SIGNED YOU UP FOR SWIMMING LESSONS.

I DON'T *WANT* SWIMMING LESSONS!!
TOO LATE. LET'S GO.

WHAT ABOUT HOBBES? DID YOU SIGN HIM UP TOO?
NO, IT'S NOT GOOD TO GET TIGERS WET.

WHY IS *THAT*?
IT TAKES US ALL DAY TO DRY, AND UNTIL WE DO, WE SMELL FUNNY.

I CAN'T BELIEVE MY MOM SIGNED ME UP FOR SWIMMING LESSONS.

HERE I AM FREEZING MY BUNS OFF AT 9 IN THE MORNING, ABOUT TO JUMP INTO ICE WATER AND DROWN.

THE ONLY THING THAT COULD POSSIBLY MAKE THIS WORSE WOULD BE IF THE CLASS WAS...

...TAUGHT BY MY SADISTIC BABY SITTER!!
WELL, LOOK WHO'S HERE!

OK... EVERYONE IN THE WATER!
I REFUSE! I'M FREEZING ALREADY!

CALVIN, DO YOU KNOW WHAT A "RAT TAIL" IS?
NO.

IT'S WHEN YOU SOAK A TOWEL AND TWIST IT UP INTO A WHIP. IT STINGS LIKE CRAZY AND IS MUCH WORSE THAN BEING COLD. GET MY DRIFT?

I ALWAYS THOUGHT LIFE-GUARDS WERE JUST TAUGHT HOW TO RESUSCITATE PEOPLE AND THINGS LIKE THAT.

THIS WATER IS FREEZING! I'M GOING TO GO INTO SHOCK AND DROWN, I JUST KNOW IT.

I BET THE LIFEGUARD IS INVOLVED IN SOME INSURANCE SCAM AND SHE'S GOING TO LET US ALL DROWN LIKE RATS! OH NO! OH NO!

OK, FIRST WE'RE GOING TO LEARN THE "DEADMAN'S FLOAT."

MOM!! HELPP! HELPP!

WHAT I PUT UP WITH TO PAY FOR COLLEGE..

I DON'T WANT TO LEARN HOW TO SWIM!

I DON'T NEED TO KNOW HOW. I'LL JUST STAY ON DRY LAND ALL MY LIFE.

WHAT IF YOU FALL OUT OF A BOAT?

NO BIG DEAL.

FORTY MINUTES OF TERROR! WHY DID YOU SIGN ME UP FOR THIS?

WHY NOT SOMETHING FUN, LIKE HANG GLIDING OR SHARPSHOOTING?

...OR *DRIVING* LESSONS! I COULD BE TAKING DRIVING LESSONS AND LEARNING SOMETHING USEFUL!

HOW ABOUT PIANO LESSONS? YOU START TUESDAY.

ACK! NO NO NO NO NO NO NO NO NO NO NO

127

THE ALIENS ARE GAINING ON OUR HERO! IN A SURPRISE MOVE, SPACEMAN SPIFF SHIFTS INTO REVERSE!

THE ALIENS ROAR AHEAD! SPIFF SHIFTS BACK INTO FORWARD, AND PURSUES THE ALIENS!

...BUT THE ALIENS HAVE TURNED AROUND AND ARE HEADED STRAIGHT FOR OUR HERO! SPIFF SHIFTS INTO REVERSE!

I'M GETTING SICK.

WHACK!

???

TELL ME THIS ISN'T A SPITBALL!!

HOBBES, QUICK! HOW DO I STOP?!?

STEER INTO A GRAVEL DRIVEWAY AND FALL DOWN!

SKRUNCH!

THAT WAS ONLY A SUGGESTION.

LOOK AT THAT THING IN THE DIRT! IT MUST BE A FOSSIL!

I WONDER WHAT PECULIAR ANIMAL *THIS* WAS.

BUT IT'S NOT A BONE. IT MUST BE SOME PRIMITIVE HUNTING WEAPON OR EATING UTENSIL FOR CAVE MEN.

MAYBE IT HAD SOME RELIGIOUS FUNCTION.

THIS EXPLAINS WHY YOUR CLOTHES STAY ON THE FLOOR.

WATTERSON

MAKING A SIGN?

I'M DECLARING THE CREEK BACK IN THE WOODS "CALVIN'S CREEK."

WHEN YOU DISCOVER SOMETHING, YOU'RE ALLOWED TO NAME IT AND PUT UP A SIGN.

Calvin's Creek

BUT SUPPOSE YOU DIDN'T DISCOVER THAT CREEK.

OF COURSE I DID! NOBODY *ELSE* HAS A SIGN THERE, RIGHT?

Hobs Crk

WATTERSON

CAN HOBBES AND I GO PLAY IN THE RAIN, MOM?

NO.

WHY NOT?

YOU'LL GET SOAKED.

WHAT'S WRONG WITH THAT?

YOU COULD CATCH PNEUMONIA, RUN UP A TERRIBLE HOSPITAL BILL, LINGER A FEW MONTHS, AND DIE.

I ALWAYS FORGET. IF YOU ASK A MOM, YOU GET A WORST-CASE SCENARIO.

I HAD NO IDEA THESE LITTLE SHOWERS WERE SO *DANGEROUS*.

WATTERSON

WHAT'S FOR DINNER?

SALMON.

SALMON?! BLECCHH!!

CALVIN, ONE OF THESE DAYS YOUR FACE IS GOING TO FREEZE LIKE THAT.

WOW!

WATTERSON

HI, HOBBES!

GOOD HEAVENS, WHAT'S WRONG WITH *YOU*?

MOM SAID IF I KEEP MAKING THIS FACE, IT WILL FREEZE LIKE THIS FOREVER!

YOU REALLY THINK SO?

IT'S WORTH A TRY...

I'LL BET MY FEATURES ARE HARDENING ALREADY.

I ALWAYS LIKED GARGOYLES.

WATTERSON

DON'T MAKE FACES AT THE TABLE, CALVIN.

I CAN'T HELP IT.

MOM SAID MY FACE WOULD FREEZE LIKE THIS SOME DAY, AND IT JUST DID.

NO, IT DIDN'T.

IT DID, DAD! MOM WAS RIGHT. I'M HORRIBLY DISFIGURED FOR LIFE.

NO, YOU AREN'T.

BUT DON'T WORRY, I WON'T SPOIL DINNER. SEE? ELEPHANT MAN!

WATTERSON

HERE COMES SUSIE.

HA! WON'T SHE BE HORRIFIED TO SEE HOW OUR FACES HAVE TRAGICALLY FROZEN!

HI, SUSIE.

HI, CALVIN.

WHAT DID YOU DO, GET YOUR HEAD STUCK IN THE BLENDER? IT'S AN IMPROVEMENT.

WATTERSON

ARE THE COALS HOT?

YES, THEY'RE VERY HOT. I'M JUST ABOUT TO PUT ON THE HAMBURGERS.

BEFORE YOU DO, COULD YOU TOSS IN THE CAN OF LIGHTER FLUID AND MAKE A GIANT FIREBALL?

I'VE GOT THE MOST BORING DAD IN THE WORLD.

WATTERSON

WITH THESE SNORKELS, WE CAN STAY UNDER WATER INDEFINITELY.

JUST THINK OF ALL THE FISH WE'LL BE ABLE TO SEE!

WE CAN COLLECT SHELLS!

LET'S GO!

WELL SO FAR, THIS HAS BEEN A MAJOR DISAPPOINTMENT.

WATTERSON

Calvin and Hobbes

by WATTERSON

YOU KNOW, DAD, IT DISTURBS ME THAT THIS WAGON HAS NO SEAT BELTS AND WOULDN'T SURVIVE A 30 MPH IMPACT WITH A STATIONARY OBJECT.

UM... WHY DO YOU BRING THIS UP?

OH, NO REASON.

WANT TO HELP ME TEST THE THEORY OF RELATIVITY?

SURE.

THE IDEA IS THAT THE FASTER WE GO, THE SLOWER TIME GOES.

GOTCHA. ITS 10:23.

WHAT TIME IS IT NOW?

10:24. GO FASTER.

WE'RE GOING PRETTY FAST! WHAT TIME IS IT?

10:25. TIME STILL HASN'T STOPPED.

HAS TIME STOPPED *NOW*?

NO, JUST MY HEART.

WELL, IT LOOKS LIKE EINSTEIN'S A FRAUD, WOULDN'T YOU SAY?

NO, HE'S RIGHT! LOOK, MY WATCH ISN'T GOING AT ALL ANY MORE!!

"ADD TWO EGGS AND STIR." RIGHT.

THE RECIPE SAYS IT MAKES TWENTY PANCAKES, SO WE'LL EACH GET TEN.

NAH, THAT'S TOO MUCH TROUBLE.

WE'LL JUST MAKE ONE *BIG* PANCAKE AND CUT IT IN HALF.

DAD, I WANT A BEDTIME STORY! I'M BUSY, CALVIN. I'LL READ YOU ONE TOMORROW.

IF YOU DON'T READ ME A STORY, I WON'T GO TO BED!

Once upon a time there was a boy named Calvin, who always wanted things his way. One day his dad got sick of it and locked him in the basement for the rest of his life. Everyone else lived happily ever after. *The End.*

I DON'T LIKE THESE STORIES WITH MORALS.

DINNER'S READY, CALVIN. COME TO THE TABLE.

I'M WATCHING TELEVISION. NO, YOU'RE NOT!

YES, I AM. I'M RIGHT HERE IN FRONT OF IT!

NO YOU'RE *NOT!* OH THAT'S RIGHT. I'M AT THE TABLE.

I SAW A TURTLE DOWN BY THE CREEK.

BIG DEAL! WHO CARES? I'VE SEEN HUNDREDS OF TURTLES! PROBABLY MILLIONS! WHO WANTS TO SEE ANOTHER DUMB OL' TURTLE?

HA!

CAN I RIDE IN THE GROCERY CART?

I THINK YOU'RE A LITTLE BIG FOR THAT NOW.

PLEASE??

ALL RIGHT. UP YOU GO.

OH BOY!

NOW RUN DOWN THE AISLE AND LET GO!

AAWWEEEAWWEEAAW!

THE WATER LOOKED A LITTLE COLD, EH, TARZAN?

Calvin and Hobbes
by WATTERSON

WANNA TOSS THE OL' PIGSKIN AROUND?

HECK NO.

PHOOEY.

THE CENTER SNAPS THE BALL!

THE QUARTERBACK LOOKS FOR AN OPENING!

THE DEFENSE DISINTEGRATES BENEATH THE COMING ONSLAUGHT! THE QUARTERBACK JUMPS AND DODGES!

HOBBES BREAKS CLEAR!

CALVIN PASSES!

AN AMAZING CATCH! HOBBES IS AT THE 30 ... THE 20... THE 10...

...BUT HE'S TACKLED FROM BEHIND AND LATERALS TO CALVIN SO *HE* CAN MAKE THE TOUCHDOWN!

BUT CALVIN FUMBLES THE BALL AND HOBBES RECOVERS IT!

BUT A PENALTY IS CALLED ON THE PLAY AND HOBBES IS SENT TO THE BENCH!

HOBBES DEFECTS TO THE OTHER TEAM AND IS GREETED WITH ENTHUSIASTIC CHEERS! THE CROWD GOES WILD!

CALVIN PREPARES TO CRIPPLE THE TRAITOR WITH AN ILLEGAL FACE MASK PULL!

HOBBES DEFIES HIM BY POURING OUT HIS MOUTH GUARD ONTO CALVIN'S HELMET!

BOY, YOU CAN SEE WHY FOOTBALL IS SUCH A VIOLENT GAME!

HOBBES' TEAM GAINS A YARD! ALL THE CHEERLEADERS COME OUT FOR SMOOCHES!!

I THINK I'M USING TOO STRONG A SUN SCREEN.

FISHING IS THE MOST BORING SPORT IN THE WORLD.

WE'VE BEEN SITTING HERE FOR TWENTY MINUTES AND NOT ONE THING HAS HAPPENED!

WAAUGHH

YOU'RE ON MY HALF OF THE BED! MOVE OVER!

YOUR SIDE IS WAY OVER THERE! GIVE ME BACK THOSE COVERS!

CALVIN, BE QUIET AND GO TO SLEEP!!

YOU HEARD DAD. HE SAID TO GET ON YOUR SIDE AND LEAVE THE COVERS ALONE!

THAT'S NOT WHAT HE SAID! *HEY!* YOU STOLE MY PILLOW! THIS LUMPY ONE IS YOURS!

WITH A DRINK OF MAGIC ELIXIR, CALVIN TURNS HIMSELF INVISIBLE.

COMPLETELY TRANSPARENT, HE ROAMS UNDETECTED!

CALVIN?

BOY, AS SOON AS YOU WANT SOMETHING DONE AROUND HERE, THAT KID'S NOWHERE TO BE SEEN.

HA HA! I HAVE TURNED MYSELF INVISIBLE!

BY REMOVING MY CLOTHING, I CAN PERPETRATE ANY CRIME UNDETECTED!

I HAVE COMPLETE FREEDOM! I CAN GET AWAY WITH ANYTHING!

CALVIN! WHAT ON EARTH ARE YOU DOING IN THE COOKIE JAR WITHOUT YOUR CLOTHES ON ?!?

YOUR POLLS ARE SLIPPING, DAD. BETTER GET WITH IT.

CALVIN, BEING YOUR DAD IS NOT AN ELECTED POSITION. I DON'T HAVE TO RESPOND TO POLLS.

NOT ELECTED? YOU MEAN YOU CAN GOVERN WITH DICTATORIAL IMPUNITY?

EXACTLY.

IN SHORT, OPEN REVOLT AND EXILE IS THE ONLY HOPE FOR CHANGE?

I DON'T LIKE THE DIRECTION THIS CONVERSATION IS TAKING..

CaLViN and HObbES

by WATTERSON

GRAVITY IS ARBITRARY!

CALVIN WAKES UP ONE DAY TO FIND HE IS IMMUNE TO THE FORCE OF GRAVITY.

HE HANGS ON TO THE GROUND FOR DEAR LIFE, BUT HIS GRIP IS WEAKENING!

HE CAN'T HOLD ON! HE... HE **LETS GO!**

HIGHER AND HIGHER, AS UPWARD HE FALLS!

ONLY BY GRABBING THE TAIL FIN OF A PASSING JET DOES CALVIN SAVE HIMSELF FROM BEING HURLED OUT INTO SPACE!

NO, NO, LET HIM FINISH. THIS IS VERY INTERESTING. SO AFTER YOU LANDED IN PHOENIX, WHAT HAPPENED?

WELL, I DON'T CARE. I'M NOT SEWING VELCRO ON THE OUTSIDE OF ALL HIS CLOTHES.

WELL, ABOUT THEN MY GRAVITY CAME BACK, SO I...

CRASH!

IT JUMPED ME!!

WATTERSON

LOOK, THERE'S A FROG!

C'MON, LET'S CATCH IT!

I'M NOT GETTING NEAR IT.

WHY NOT?

THEY DRINK WATER ALL DAY JUST IN CASE SOMEONE PICKS THEM UP.

WATTERSON

I'M GOING TO HANG AROUND THE DRUGSTORE ALL AFTERNOON AND EAT CANDY AND READ COMIC BOOKS!

OH, NO, YOU'RE NOT!

WHY NOT?!

WATTERSON

BECAUSE I'M YOUR MOTHER AND I SAID SO. GET BACK IN HERE.

AND YOU CAN STOP GOOSE-STEPPING AROUND THE HOUSE!

HEY, MOM, CAN WE GO OUT FOR PIZZA TONIGHT?

NO, WE HAD PIZZA LAST NIGHT, AND BESIDES, IT'S TOO EXPENSIVE TO EAT OUT ALL THE TIME.

OH, YOU'D RATHER BLOW THE EVENING COOKING AND WASHING DISHES THAN SPEND A FEW BUCKS?

IT SEEMS LIKE WE GO OUT FOR PIZZA A LOT THESE DAYS.

IF YOU'D RATHER FIX A DISH OF CEREAL AT HOME, BE MY GUEST.

HOBBES WANTS TRIPLE ANCHOVIES.

CALVIN AND HIS TRUSTY NAVIGATOR HOBBES ROAR DOWN THE RESIDENTIAL ROAD AT 90 M.P.H.!

HOBBES PUTS ON THE TURN SIGNAL.

FASTER AND FASTER THEY GO! A BUSLOAD OF SCHOOLCHILDREN DIVES FROM THE SIDEWALK!

HOBBES PUTS ON THE WINDSHIELD WIPERS.

THE POLICE ARE AFTER THEM! CALVIN CRAWLS DOWN TO PUT IN THE CLUTCH AND SHIFT!

HOBBES STEERS AND BLOWS THE HORN!

ALL RIGHT, I'M BACK ALREADY! CAN'T I EVEN RUN AN ERRAND WITHOUT YOU BLOWING THE HORN ACROSS THE PARKING LOT?!

IT WAS HOBBES, MOM. NOT ME.

SEE ANY UFOs?

NOT YET.

WELL, KEEP YOUR EYES PEELED. THEY'RE BOUND TO LAND HERE SOONER OR LATER.

WHAT WILL WE DO WHEN THEY COME?

SEE IF WE CAN SELL MOM AND DAD INTO SLAVERY FOR A STAR CRUISER.

SUMMER VACATION'S OVER! NOTHING AHEAD BUT TOIL AND DRUDGERY FOR A WHOLE YEAR!

OH, COME ON, YOU SPENT HALF THE SUMMER COMPLAINING HOW BORED YOU WERE.

I DID?

YOU DID.

HOW STRANGE. I MUST HAVE BEEN DELIRIOUS FROM HAVING SO MUCH FUN.

I CAN'T BELIEVE IT! HOMEWORK ALREADY! I JUST GOT BACK TO SCHOOL!

I HAVE TO WRITE A PARAGRAPH ON WHAT I DID OVER THE SUMMER! *A WHOLE PARAGRAPH!!*

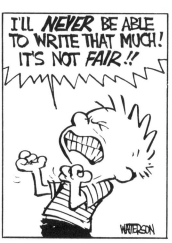

I'LL *NEVER* BE ABLE TO WRITE THAT MUCH! IT'S NOT *FAIR*!!

HOW'S IT COMING?

NOT SO GOOD. WHAT DID YOU DO BESIDES WATCH TV?

IN SOCCER, YOU CAN'T TOUCH THE BALL WITH YOUR HANDS OR ARMS.

SEE, YOU CAN USE ANY OTHER PART OF YOUR BODY...

...EVEN YOUR HEAD!

YEAH, BUT YOUR *FACE*?? DOESN'T THAT *HURT*?

RRRRGHH! THAT'S *NOT* WHAT I MEANT TO *DO*!

I HAVE A HYPOTHETICAL QUESTION. SUPPOSE A KID AT SCHOOL CALLED ME A NASTY NAME...

...SHOULD I KICK HIM REAL HARD IN THE SHINS?

NO, I DON'T THINK VIOLENCE WOULD BE JUSTIFIED.

HERE'S ANOTHER HYPOTHETICAL QUESTION. WHAT IF I ALREADY DID?

I'VE DECIDED TO GROW A BEARD, MOM.

A *LONG* BEARD. LIKE THE GUYS IN ZZ TOP.

THAT'S NICE, CALVIN. YOU GO AHEAD AND DO THAT.

I THOUGHT SHE'D PUT UP MORE OF A FUSS THAN THAT.

HOW ABOUT THESE PANTS, MOM? CAN I GET THESE?

GOOD HEAVENS, LOOK AT THE PRICE! *I* DON'T HAVE PANTS THAT COST THIS MUCH!

AND YOU'LL GROW RIGHT OUT OF THESE! HONESTLY, WHY WOULD ANY KID NEED DESIGNER CLOTHES??

"BABES."

BABES, MOM. I GOTTA LOOK COOL.

Hey, Twinkie, here's the 25¢ I "borrowed" from you the other day.

Somebody ratted on me, and it's gonna be a dark day if I ever find out who!

I THINK I'LL USE THE QUARTER TO CALL MY INSURANCE AGENT.

HI, DAD, IT'S ME!

CALVIN, IS THIS IMPORTANT? I'M VERY BUSY THIS MORNING.

I'LL MAKE IT FAST, DAD. CAN YOU PICK UP SOME TOPSOIL AND GRASS SEED ON YOUR WAY HOME?

OK, SURE. GOODBYE.

RING RING

HELLO, CALVIN SPEAKING. I'D LIKE TO ORDER A LARGE ANCHOVY PIZZA.

WHAT? I...??

OH, I'M SORRY. YOU MUST HAVE DIALED THE WRONG NUMBER. GOODBYE.

I TRY TO MAKE EVERYONE'S DAY A LITTLE MORE SURREAL.

Calvin and Hobbes

by WATTERSON

QUIT SQUIRMING, CALVIN. YOU'VE GOT ICE CREAM ALL OVER YOUR SHIRT.

RATS, I WAS SAVING IT FOR LATER.

THANKS FOR THE ICE CREAM, DAD. IT WAS GREAT.

YOU'RE WELCOME.

I'M TIRED OF PULLING YOU. IT'S *MY* TURN TO RIDE.

YOUR DAD DIDN'T GET ME ANY ICE CREAM, SO I GET TO RIDE BOTH WAYS.

NO, YOU DON'T! DAD SAID TIGERS DON'T *LIKE* ICE CREAM! IT'S MY TURN TO RIDE!

TIGERS DON'T KNOW IF THEY LIKE ICE CREAM UNTIL THEY TRY EVERY KIND. I'M NOT PULLING.

I'VE GOT NEWS, FUZZ BRAIN. I'M NOT PULLING, EITHER!

WELL THEN, I GUESS WE'LL BOTH JUST SIT HERE UNTIL WE DIE.

WHY DO THESE "WALKS" ALWAYS END UP AS "RIDES"?

OH, YOU NEED THE EXERCISE MORE ANYWAY.

154

156

WITH GREAT EFFORT, CALVIN THE HUMAN INSECT ADVANCES THE PAPER IN THE TYPEWRITER.

HIS ONLY HOPE FOR PROPER MEDICAL TREATMENT LIES IN HIS ABILITY TO WRITE A LEGIBLE MESSAGE TO HIS FAMILY!

HE CRAWLS TO EACH KEY AND JUMPS!

WHO WROTE "HELP I'M A BUG" ON MY LETTER TO GRANDMA?

EVIDENTLY SOME BUG. HOW STRANGE.

BACK AND FORTH.

BACK AND FORTH.

TIDAL WAVE!

BEATS ME, MOM. MAYBE THE SEAL AROUND THE TUB LEAKS.

WHAT'S THIS MUSIC?

IT'S "THE 1812 OVERTURE."

I KINDA LIKE IT. INTERESTING PERCUSSION SECTION.

THOSE ARE CANNONS.

AND THEY PERFORM THIS IN CROWDED CONCERT HALLS?? GEE, I THOUGHT CLASSICAL MUSIC WAS BORING!

BOY, WHAT A DAY!

I WENT TO SCHOOL, PLAYED OUTSIDE, AND DID MY HOMEWORK. I'M EXHAUSTED.

YOU KNOW WHAT TIME IT IS NOW?

UH, 7:35.

IT'S MILLER TIME.

GET BACK HERE.

PSST... SUSIE! WHAT'S 12 + 7?

A BILLION.

THANKS!

WAIT A MINUTE. THAT CAN'T BE RIGHT...

THAT'S WHAT SHE SAID 3+4 WAS.

I JUST READ THIS GREAT SCIENCE FICTION STORY.

IT'S ABOUT HOW MACHINES TAKE CONTROL OF HUMANS AND TURN THEM INTO ZOMBIE SLAVES!

SO INSTEAD OF US CONTROLLING MACHINES, THEY CONTROL US? PRETTY SCARY IDEA.

I'LL SAY. *HEY!* WHAT TIME IS IT?? MY TV SHOW IS ON!

TOMORROW WE'RE GOING TO DISCUSS "CURRENT EVENTS" IN SCHOOL.

EACH OF US HAS TO FIND A NEWSPAPER ARTICLE, READ IT TO THE CLASS, AND EXPLAIN IT.

WHAT ARTICLE DID YOU CHOOSE?

THIS ONE.

"SPACE ALIEN WEDS TWO-HEADED ELVIS CLONE."

ACTUALLY, THERE'S NOT MUCH LEFT TO EXPLAIN.

LOOK WHAT YOU CAN DO WITH BIG SOCKS!

JUST PUT ONE OVER EACH EAR, AND ONE OVER YOUR NOSE...

AN ELEPHANT! HA HA! I WANT SOME SOCKS TOO!

IF I MISS THE BUS, IT'S GOING TO BE UNPLEASANT AROUND HERE!

CALVIN, HOW DID YOU BREAK THIS DISH?!

I WAS CARRYING TOO MUCH AND IT DROPPED.

YOUR PROBLEM IS YOU'VE GOT NO COMMON SENSE.

I'VE GOT **PLENTY** OF COMMON SENSE!

I JUST CHOOSE TO IGNORE IT.

I DON'T UNDERSTAND THIS BUSINESS ABOUT DEATH.

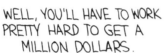
IF WE'RE JUST GOING TO DIE, WHAT'S THE POINT OF LIVING?

WELL, THERE'S SEAFOOD...

I DON'T KNOW WHY I EVEN *TALK* TO YOU BEFORE DINNER.

I'VE DECIDED I WANT TO BE A MILLIONAIRE WHEN I GROW UP.

WELL, YOU'LL HAVE TO WORK PRETTY HARD TO GET A MILLION DOLLARS.

NO, I WON'T. YOU WILL.

ME?

I JUST WANT TO INHERIT IT.

THE WORST PART ABOUT GOING TO SCHOOL IS WAITING FOR THE BUS.

ALL YOU CAN DO IS STAND HERE AND IMAGINE WHAT'S GOING TO GO WRONG DURING THE DAY. I BET WE HAVE A POP MATH QUIZ OR SOMETHING.

WELL, HERE COMES THE BUS. THANKS FOR WAITING WITH ME.

MY PLEASURE.

BOY, MY LUNCH BOX SEEMS LIGHT.

AS YOU CAN SEE, SPACEMAN SPIFF, WE HAVE WAYS OF EXTRACTING INFORMATION FROM EVEN THE MOST UNCOOPERATIVE PRISONERS!

OUR HERO, CAPTURED BY ZORKONS, EYES THE DIABOLICAL INSTRUMENTS OF TORTURE!

VERY AMUSING, YOU TWISTED SPACE FROG. WHAT'S *THIS* FIENDISH DEVICE CALLED?

A CHIN-UP BAR. GET ON IT.

SPIFF READIES HIS DARING ESCAPE...

WHERE'S MY JACKET?

IT'S RIGHT ON THE FLOOR WHERE YOU LEFT IT.

IT'S STILL ON THE FLOOR? WHY DIDN'T YOU PUT IT AWAY?

GEE, MY OWN COPY OF THE EMANCIPATION PROCLAMATION.

LOOK, I CAN MAKE SHADOWS ON THE WALL. HERE'S A DOG.

HEY, THAT'S GOOD!

HERE'S A SWAN.

HMM... THAT LOOKS MORE LIKE SOME BUG-EYED TENTACLED THING...

MOMMM!

LOOK, MOM, I PUT ALL MY CLOTHES FOR TOMORROW ON THE STAIRS.

THEN IN THE MORNING, I'LL RUN OUT IN MY UNDERWEAR AND SLIDE DOWN AT TOP SPEED!

IF I AIM GOOD, I GO RIGHT INTO MY PANTS WHILE I'M PUTTING ON MY SHIRT, AND BY THE BOTTOM, I'M ALL DRESSED FOR SCHOOL!

AND IF YOU PUT MY CEREAL ON THE STAIRS TOO, I WON'T HAVE TO GET UP UNTIL 30 SECONDS BEFORE THE BUS COMES.

FORGET IT, CALVIN.

WATTERSON

ACK   IGG

LOOK, MOM, I'VE GOT RABIES.

GO SPIT OUT YOUR TOOTHPASTE AND STOP BEING SILLY.

MAYBE DAD WILL FALL FOR IT IF I BITE HIM FIRST.

WATTERSON

WHAT ARE YOU GOING TO DRESS UP AS FOR HALLOWEEN?

I DON'T KNOW YET. I CAN'T DECIDE.

WATTERSON

WELL, THE IDEA IS TO BE THE SCARIEST THING YOU CAN THINK OF.

HMM...MAYBE I'LL JUST GO AS MYSELF!

I'M GOING AS A BARREL OF TOXIC WASTE!

WE'RE GOING TO CARVE A JACK-O'-LANTERN NOW.

SEE, WE'LL MAKE A FACE ON THIS PUMPKIN SO IT WILL LOOK LIKE A HEAD.

BUT FIRST WE HAVE TO OPEN UP THE TOP AND SCOOP OUT THE GLOP INSIDE.

OK, JACK, TIME FOR YOUR LOBOTOMY!!

HAND ME A BIG SPOON, WILL YOU, HOBBES?

UGH! NO ANESTHETIC EVEN.

WATTERSON

I THINK DAD LIKES HALLOWEEN AS MUCH AS WE DO.

IS HE TAKING US TRICK OR TREATING TONIGHT?

NO, MOM IS.

IS HE GOING TO STAY HOME AND GIVE OUT CANDY?

WATTERSON

NO, HE'S GOING TO SIT IN THE BUSHES WITH THE GARDEN HOSE AND DRENCH POTENTIAL T.P. ERS.

OOG, I FEEL AWFUL.

IF SOMEONE EVEN MENTIONS "MILK DUDS," I'M GONNA BARF.

WATTERSON

ANOTHER HALLOWEEN COME AND GONE.

IT'S ALWAYS SUCH A LETDOWN AFTER A HOLIDAY.

WE MIGHT AS WELL GO INTO TOWN AND LOOK AT THE CHRISTMAS DECORATIONS.

MOM'S NOT FEELING WELL, SO I'M MAKING HER A "GET WELL" CARD.

THAT'S THOUGHTFUL OF YOU.

SEE, ON THE FRONT IT SAYS, "GET WELL SOON."

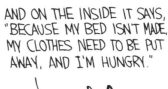

AND ON THE INSIDE IT SAYS, "BECAUSE MY BED ISN'T MADE, MY CLOTHES NEED TO BE PUT AWAY, AND I'M HUNGRY."

"LOVE, CALVIN." WANT TO SIGN IT?

SURE. I'M HUNGRY TOO.

HI, MOM! SINCE YOU'RE SICK, I'M BRINGING YOU BREAKFAST IN BED!

I PREPARED EGGS, TOAST AND ORANGE JUICE FOR YOU ALL BY MYSELF!

HOW NICE!

THE EGGS KIND OF BURNED AND STUCK TO THE PAN, BUT YOU CAN PROBABLY CHIP THEM OUT WITH THIS CHISEL.

UM... WHERE IS THE TOAST AND ORANGE JUICE?

DAD SAID NOT TO TELL YOU ABOUT THAT TILL YOU'RE BETTER.

SINCE YOUR MOM'S SICK, I'LL BE MAKING DINNER TONIGHT.

YOU CAN COOK?

OF COURSE I CAN COOK.

AS YOU CAN SEE, I SURVIVED TWO YEARS OF MY OWN COOKING WHEN I HAD AN APARTMENT AFTER COLLEGE.

MOM SAYS YOU ATE FROZEN WAFFLES AND CANNED SOUP THREE MEALS A DAY.

YOUR MOM WASN'T THERE, SO SHE WOULDN'T KNOW. GET THE SYRUP OUT, WILL YOU?

SOMETIMES WHEN *I'M* SICK, YOU READ ME A STORY. WANT ME TO READ *YOU* ONE?

NO, THANKS, CALVIN. I JUST WANT TO REST.

IT'S HARD TO BE A MOM FOR A MOM.

YOU DO FINE, SWEETIE.

WHOA! HEY! ARE YOU CONTAGIOUS?!

WHAT'S WRONG WITH YOUR MOM, DO YOU KNOW?

NO. SHE WENT TO THE DOCTOR TODAY, THOUGH.

I WONDER IF... NAH.

WHAT?

YOU DON'T SUPPOSE SHE'S GOING TO HAVE A BABY, DO YOU?

A BABY?!?

WHY WOULD SHE WANT ANOTHER KID?? SHE'S ALREADY GOT *ME!*

YES, YOU'D THINK SHE'D HAVE LEARNED HER LESSON...

I ASKED DAD IF MOM WAS GOING TO HAVE A BABY, AND HE SAID NOT THAT *HE* KNEW OF.

DAD SAID WE'D KNOW IF MOM WAS HAVING A KID BECAUSE SHE'D LOOK LIKE A HIPPOPOTAMUS WITH A GLAND PROBLEM.

...THAT'S WHEN MOM CREAMED HIM WITH HER PILLOW.

DAD SAYS SHE MUST BE FEELING BETTER.

YOU HAVE WEIRD PARENTS.

HEY, MOM, I GOT A PART IN THE CLASS PLAY!

I GET TO SAY A LINE, AND EVERYTHING!

THAT'S WONDERFUL, CALVIN.

IT'S A GREAT DRAMATIC ROLE! MY CHARACTER WILL HAVE EVERYONE IN TEARS AT THE END OF THE SECOND ACT!

WHAT'S THE PLAY?

"NUTRITION AND THE FOUR FOOD GROUPS." I'M AN ONION.

OK, HOBBES, I NEED YOU TO HELP ME MEMORIZE MY LINE FOR THE PLAY.

SURE.

I'M THE ONION, AND I SAY, "IN ADDITION TO SUPPLYING VITAL NUTRIENTS, MANY VEGETABLES ARE A SOURCE OF DIETARY FIBER."

OK, READY?

READY. GO AHEAD. "IN ADDITION..."

WAIT. HOLD IT. I'M NOT IN CHARACTER YET. WHAT MOTIVATES AN ONION?

FAME, I SUPPOSE. THIS COULD BE A BIG BREAK.

OK, YOU BE "BREAD." PROMPT ME.

"GLUCOSE IS THE BODY'S MAIN ENERGY SOURCE!"

"IN ADDITION..." UH... UM... "IN ADDITION..." UM... WAIT..

GRRRGHH! I HATE THIS PLAY! I'LL NEVER BE ABLE TO LEARN THIS STUPID PART!

WELL, YOUR EMOTING IS DOWN PAT.

I'VE GOT IT ALL FIGURED OUT, HOBBES. THIS PLAY WILL BE NO SWEAT.

YOU HAVE YOUR LINE ALL MEMORIZED?

NO, I THOUGHT I'D COME OUT, DO A LITTLE SOFT-SHOE, AND AD-LIB SOMETHING!

AD-LIB SOMETHING ABOUT DIETARY FIBER?

EITHER THAT, OR I'LL DO MY ONION IN MIME!

HOW'S MY ONION COSTUME COMING, MOM?

I'M STILL WORKING ON IT. I WISH YOUR CLASS WOULD DO SOMETHING A LITTLE LESS ELABORATE. I'M NOT MUCH OF A SEAMSTRESS.

JUST BE GLAD I'M NOT RUSSY WHITE. *HE* HAS TO BE AN AMINO ACID.

MM... WHAT DO YOU THINK?

JABBA THE HUTT MEETS RUDOLF THE REINDEER. I DUNNO, MOM.

ARE YOU GOING TO COME TO MY PLAY, DAD? IT'S CALLED "NUTRITION AND THE FOUR FOOD GROUPS."

I'LL PROBABLY HAVE TO BE AT WORK, CALVIN.

BUT DAD, IT'LL BE GREAT DRAMA! I'M AN ONION!

WELL, WHY DON'T YOU SAY YOUR LINE FOR ME NOW?

OK! UM... ..LET'S SEE.. "IN ADDITION TO..." .. UH... HOLD IT... UM..

25 KIDS IN FOOD SUITS, FORGETTING THEIR LINES. I'LL *DEFINITELY* BE AT WORK.

DEAR! CALVIN'S WORKED HARD.

OK, UH... "IN ADDITION.."..UH NO, WAIT.. UM...

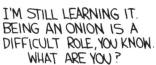

DO YOU HAVE YOUR LINE MEMORIZED FOR THE NUTRITION PLAY, CALVIN?

I'M STILL LEARNING IT. BEING AN ONION IS A DIFFICULT ROLE, YOU KNOW. WHAT ARE YOU?

I'M "FAT."

NO, I MEAN IN THE PLAY.

ANYONE *ELSE* WANT TO SAY IT ?!?

AACKK! UNDERSTUDY! UNDERSTUDY!

THANKS FOR WAITING FOR THE BUS WITH ME, HOBBES. I FEEL LIKE AN IDIOT IN THIS ONION SUIT.

I'LL BE GLAD WHEN THIS STUPID PLAY IS OVER.

OH NO! RUN FOR YOUR LIFE! A PRODUCE TRUCK!

...JUST KIDDING!

SUSIE, WHERE'S CALVIN? HE GOES ONSTAGE RIGHT AFTER YOU!

I DON'T KNOW, MISS WORMWOOD. HE WAS HERE A MINUTE AGO.

MAYBE HE WENT TO THE BOYS' ROOM.

HE'S ON IN TWO MINUTES! FINE TIME TO GO TO THE BOYS' ROOM!

FINE TIME TO GET STUCK IN MY COSTUME. STUPID ZIPPER!

I CAN'T BELIEVE IT! I'M STUCK IN MY ONION SUIT!

I CAN'T GO ONSTAGE WITH MY SHIRT CAUGHT IN MY COSTUME! HELP! HELP!

I'M SUPPOSED TO BE ON NOW! I'M SUPPOSED TO BE SAYING MY LINE! WHAT SHOULD I DO?? WHAT SHOULD I DO??

"IN ADDITION TO SUPPLYING VITAL NUTRIENTS, MANY VEGETABLES ARE A SOURCE OF DIETARY FIBER!!"

WATTERSON

I'M HOME!

HI, HONEY. HOW DID YOUR PLAY GO?

TERRIBLE. I GOT STUCK IN MY ZIPPER IN THE BATHROOM, AND THEY HAD TO STOP THE PLAY AND GET A JANITOR TO FIND ME AND GET ME OUT.

OH NO. THAT'S AWFUL!

I'LL SAY... THE PLAY WAS RUINED.

...BUT I REMEMBERED MY LINE!

WATTERSON

UP, UP AND AWAY!

WOOMPH!

ACKK! KRYPTONITE! KRYPTONITE!

WATTERSON

Calvin and Hobbes by WATTERSON

OP ZIP ZOP ZIP ZOP ZIP ZOP ZIP ZOP ZIP ZOP ZIP ZOP

WANT TO TRADE SANDWICHES, CALVIN?

NO, I'VE GOT MY FAVORITE KIND. WHAT DID YOU BRING?

PEANUT BUTTER.

I HAVE PROCESSED MOUSE LOAF.

OH, GROSS. THAT'S NOT REALLY MOUSE LOAF. IT LOOKS LIKE EGG SALAD.

TASTE IT AND SEE. HERE, I THINK THIS IS A WHISKER. IT'S GOOD.

FORGET IT. I DON'T EVEN WANT MY *OWN* LUNCH ANY MORE.

YOU DON'T? WHAT KIND OF COOKIES ARE THOSE?

TRIP!

TA-DAAA!!

HOW DO THEY KNOW THE LOAD LIMIT ON BRIDGES, DAD?

LOAD LIMIT 10 TONS

THEY DRIVE BIGGER AND BIGGER TRUCKS OVER THE BRIDGE UNTIL IT BREAKS.

THEN THEY WEIGH THE LAST TRUCK AND REBUILD THE BRIDGE.

OH. I SHOULD'VE GUESSED.

DEAR, IF YOU DON'T KNOW THE ANSWER, JUST TELL HIM!

IT'S HARD TO BELIEVE PEOPLE STILL STARVE IN THIS WORLD.

THERE'S EVEN HUNGER IN AMERICA.

SOME PEOPLE NEVER GET ENOUGH TO EAT.

BOY, I KNOW WHAT *THAT'S* LIKE!

NO YOU DON'T.

WATTERSON

THE SOLDIERS ADVANCE UP THE HILL!

OH, NO! A SQUADRON OF BOMBERS APPEARS ON THE HORIZON! THE BOMBS BEGIN TO FALL!

BONK BONK

TWO DIRECT HITS!

I SEE YOU UP THERE!

WATTERSON

LOOK, HOBBES, YOU GET A PLASTIC TRINKET IN BOXES OF "CHOCOLATE-FROSTED SUGAR BOMBS"!

IT SAYS, "BE THE FIRST IN YOUR NEIGHBORHOOD TO COLLECT ALL TEN COLORS."

YEAH, BUT MOM SAYS SHE WON'T BUY ANY MORE CEREAL UNTIL THIS BOX IS GONE.

THAT SHOULDN'T TAKE MORE THAN A COUPLE HOURS, RIGHT?

I DUNNO. AFTER FIVE BOWLS, I GET PRETTY WIRED.

WATTERSON

CALVIN, YOUR DAD AND I ARE GOING OUT TOMORROW, SO YOU'LL BE HAVING A BABY SITTER.

OH NO! NOT ROSALYN!

I CALLED EIGHT PEOPLE AND SHE'S THE ONLY ONE WHO WOULD DO IT.

CALL SOME MORE! CALL SOME MORE!

CALVIN, I SPENT AN HOUR ON THE PHONE ALREADY. ROSALYN'S FINE.

"FINE"?? SHE'S A BARRACUDA IN A HIGH SCHOOL SENIOR SUIT! I'M AS GOOD AS DEAD!

YOU REMEMBER AMY? SHE JUST LAUGHED WHEN I CALLED HER.

OH NO! A KNOCK AT THE DOOR! THE BABY SITTER MUST BE HERE!

SHOULD WE HIDE?

NO WAY. BABY SITTERS CAN SMELL FEAR IN LITTLE KIDS. WE'D BE DOOMED.

SO WE GO ON THE OFFENSIVE?

RIGHT. HERE'S A NOTEPAD AND PENCIL.

OH BOY, BLACKMAIL!

RIGHT. GET TO THE UPSTAIRS PHONE WHEN SHE CALLS HER BOYFRIEND.

WE'RE GOING, ROSALYN. HELP YOURSELF TO ANYTHING IN THE FRIDGE.

OK, GOOD-BYE.

CALVIN? ARE YOU UPSTAIRS?

WAP WAP

ALL RIGHT, KID! BEDTIME FOR BONZO!!

WHAT?! GET AWAY! IT'S NOT EVEN 6 O'CLOCK!

I CAN'T BELIEVE OUR BABY SITTER PUT US TO BED! IT'S NOT EVEN DARK OUT!

WELL, SHE CAN PUT US TO BED, BUT SHE CAN'T MAKE US SLEEP. YOU PLAY THE HORN, AND I'LL ACCOMPANY ON TOM-TOM.

CALVIN, I JUST WANTED TO REMIND YOU THAT SLEEPING IN A BED IS A *PRIVILEGE*. THE BASEMENT IS SURE TO BE A LOT LESS COMFY.

WHAT DID SHE MEAN, "THE BASEMENT"?

SHHH!

WATTERSON

ROSALYN, WE'RE GOING TO BE A LITTLE LATER THAN WE EXPECTED, SO I THOUGHT I'D BETTER CALL YOU.

THAT'S FINE. CALVIN WENT TO BED EARLY, SO I'M JUST HOLDING DOWN THE FORT.

WHO'S ON THE PHONE? IS IT MY MOM? I WANT TO TALK TO HER! MOM! MOM! CAN YOU HEAR ME?!

COME HOME NOW BEFORE IT'S TOO LATE! HELP! HELP!

NO, THAT'S JUST THE TV. I'LL SEE YOU AT 11:30 THEN. ENJOY THE PLAY.

WATTERSON

SORRY WE'RE LATE, ROSALYN. DID YOU GET CALVIN TO BED?

YES, BUT...

MOM! DAD! IS THAT YOU? I'M NOT ASLEEP! DID YOU GET RID OF THE BABY SITTER? THANK GOODNESS YOU'RE HOME!

HAS HE BEEN THIS WAY ALL NIGHT?

WELL, HIS VOICE GAVE OUT ABOUT 11 O'CLOCK, BUT IT SEEMS TO BE.

IF SHE'S STILL HERE, DON'T PAY HER!

GIVE HER A LITTLE EXTRA, WILL YOU, DEAR?

IS FIVE ENOUGH?

COULD YOU MAKE IT EIGHT? COLLEGE TUITIONS ARE UP.

I'VE GOT A GREAT IDEA FOR SCHOOL TOMORROW.

I CUT A PING-PONG BALL IN HALF, AND NOW I'M DRAWING DOTS ON EACH END.

I'LL JUST PUT ONE OVER EACH EYE, AND IT WILL LOOK LIKE I'M REALLY PAYING ATTENTION.

...OR WILL I LOOK *TOO* INTERESTED?

I DOUBT IT. I'M OVER HERE.

BAD NEWS ON YOUR POLLS, DAD.

YOU SLIPPED ANOTHER TWO NOTCHES. THINGS ARE LOOKING GRIM FOR FUTURE OFFICE.

IS THAT SO?

ANY IDEAS ON WHAT WOULD IMPROVE MY STANDINGS?

I NEED A VCR.

RIGHT. I'LL KEEP THAT IN MIND.

I HOPE YOU'RE READING THE "HELP WANTED" SECTION.

LOOK, I GOT A LETTER I'M SUPPOSED TO COPY AND SEND TO 20 PEOPLE FOR GOOD LUCK.

IT'S A CHAIN LETTER.

IT SAYS, "A MAN IN DENVER MADE 20 COPIES AND THE NEXT DAY HE GOT A RAISE. A MAN IN SEATTLE BROKE THE CHAIN AND HE WENT BALD."

HA! YOU BELIEVE THAT? THESE LETTERS ARE FOR SUPERSTITIOUS NINCOMPOOPS. THROW IT AWAY.

"...AND A DUMB KID LIKE YOU LISTENED TO A FRIEND AND GOT RUN OVER BY A CEMENT MIXER."

Calvin and Hobbes by WATTERSON

I'M READY FOR BED, DAD. WHAT'S TONIGHT'S STORY GOING TO BE?

HERE'S ONE. "READINGS ON DIALECTICAL METAPHYSICS." YOU'LL LOVE IT.

FORGET IT, DAD. YOU CAN'T GET ME TO DROP OFF *THAT* EASY.

WILL YOU READ US *THIS* STORY? HOBBES WROTE IT HIMSELF.

HOBBES WROTE IT, HUH?

"GOLDILOCKS AND THE THREE TIGERS."

OH BOY, THIS IS GONNA BE GREAT!

"ONCE UPON A TIME THERE LIVED A YOUNG GIRL NAMED GOLDILOCKS. SHE WENT INTO THE FOREST AND SAW A COTTAGE. NO ONE WAS HOME SO SHE WENT IN."

"INSIDE SHE SAW THREE BOWLS OF PORRIDGE. A BIG BOWL, A MEDIUM BOWL, AND A SMALL BOWL. SHE WAS JUST ABOUT TO TASTE THE PORRIDGE WHEN THE THREE TIGERS CAME HOME."

"THEY QUICKLY DIVIDED GOLDILOCKS INTO BIG, MEDIUM, AND SMALL PIECES AND DUNKED THEM IN THE PORRIDGE THAT..."

CALVIN, I'M NOT GOING TO FINISH THIS! THIS IS DISGUSTING!!

I DON'T KNOW WHY I LET YOU TALK ME INTO THIS. *GOOD NIGHT!*

CLICK

HE DIDN'T EVEN LOOK AT OUR ILLUSTRATIONS.

NOW I'M ALL HUNGRY.

CALVIN HAS MYSTERIOUSLY SHRUNK TO THE SIZE OF AN INSECT!

HIS ONLY HOPE IS TO CALL FOR HELP! PUSHING WITH ALL HIS MIGHT, CALVIN DIALS THE GIGANTIC TELEPHONE!

IT'S RINGING! HE RUNS TO THE MOUTHPIECE! WILL ANYONE BE ABLE TO HEAR HIM??

BZZ BZ! BZZZZ! BZZ BZZ! BZZZ BZ!

CALVIN, THIS HAD BETTER NOT BE YOU.

WATTERSON

FWOOSHHH

GREETINGS, EARTH FEMALE. DO NOT BE ALARMED.

OUR PLANET IS DYING. WE NEED COOKIES TO SURVIVE. DO NOT TRY TO RESIST OR YOU WILL BE DESTROYED.

WE'LL SEE ABOUT THAT. GET BACK HERE.

WHY DO I HAVE TO GO TO BED NOW? I NEVER GET TO DO WHAT I WANT!

IF I GROW UP TO BE SOME SORT OF PSYCHOPATH BECAUSE OF THIS, YOU'LL ALL BE SORRY!!

WATTERSON

NOBODY EVER BECAME A PSYCHOPATH BECAUSE HE HAD TO GO TO BED AT A REASONABLE HOUR.

YEAH, BUT YOU WON'T LET ME CHEW TOBACCO EITHER! YOU NEVER KNOW WHAT MIGHT PUSH ME OVER THE BRINK!

GO TO BED, CALVIN.

OH BOY, YOU GOT SOME CLAY.

I'M MAKING MOM AND DAD A CHRISTMAS PRESENT.

WHAT ARE YOU MAKING?

AN ASHTRAY.

YOUR PARENTS DON'T SMOKE, OF COURSE...

OK, MICHELANGELO, *YOU* SCULPT SOMETHING!

A HOMEMADE GIFT SAYS MORE THAN A STORE-BOUGHT GIFT.

IT SAYS YOU CARE ENOUGH TO INVEST YOUR TIME AND SKILL IN IT.

IT SAYS THIS IS A PERSONAL GIFT, NOT A GENERIC ONE.

IT SAYS YOU NEED A BIGGER ALLOWANCE.

THIS ARTICLE SAYS THAT MANY PEOPLE FIND CHRISTMAS THE MOST STRESSFUL TIME OF YEAR.

I BELIEVE IT. THIS SEASON SURE FILLS *ME* WITH STRESS.

REALLY? HOW COME?

I HATE BEING GOOD.

PSST! ARE YOU AWAKE?

IS IT CHRISTMAS? IT IS! IT IS!

LET'S GO WAKE MOM AND DAD AND OPEN ALL OUR LOOT!

SINCE IT'S CHRISTMAS, MAYBE WE SHOULD LET THEM SLEEP IN A LITTLE.

THAT'S LONG ENOUGH! WAKE UP! WAKE UP! IT'S CHRISTMAS!!

QUARTER TO 6. HE LET US SLEEP IN THIS YEAR.

OMIGOSH! THIS LIBRARY BOOK WAS DUE TWO DAYS AGO!

WHAT WILL THEY *DO*? ARE THEY GOING TO INTERROGATE ME AND BEAT ME UP?! ARE THEY GOING TO BREAK MY KNEES?? WILL I HAVE TO SIGN SOME CONFESSION???

THEY'LL FINE YOU TEN CENTS. NOW GO RETURN IT.

THE WAY SOME OF THOSE LIBRARIANS LOOK AT YOU, I NATURALLY ASSUMED THE CONSEQUENCES WOULD BE MORE DIRE.

HEY DAD, I HAVE A QUESTION.

SURE, CALVIN. WHAT DO YOU WANT TO KNOW?

IF YOU PLUGGED UP YOUR NOSE AND MOUTH RIGHT BEFORE YOU SNEEZED...

...WOULD THE SNEEZE GO OUT YOUR EARS, OR WOULD YOUR HEAD EXPLODE?

I WAS KIND OF HOPING YOU HAD A MATH PROBLEM OR SOMETHING.

...EITHER WAY, I'M SCARED TO TRY IT.

Calvin and Hobbes
by WATTERSON

Hobbes: TOBOGGANS GIVE BETTER RIDES THAN RUNNER SLEDS.

Hobbes: WHY IS THAT?

Calvin: THERE'S NO WAY TO STEER.

Calvin: ON THESE CLOUDY WINTER DAYS, SOMETIMES I LIKE TO LIE BACK ON MY SLED AND LOOK AT THE SKY.

Calvin: IT'S JUST GRAY AND SILENT. NO BIRDS SINGING OR BUGS BUZZING. EVERYTHING IS MUFFLED BY THE SNOW.

Calvin: IMAGINE WHAT IT WOULD BE LIKE WITHOUT ANY PEOPLE OR HOUSES AROUND. IT WOULD BE PERFECTLY STILL.

WATTERSON

Calvin: PRETTY NEAT, HUH?

Hobbes: YES, VERY PEACEFUL.

Calvin: I HATE ALL THAT SILENCE.

BEHOLD THE DREADED TOBOGGAN: SUICIDE SLED.

ITS UNIQUE DESIGN SENDS A BLINDING SPRAY OF SNOW ON ITS PASSENGERS AT THE SLIGHTEST BUMP. NOTE, TOO, THE LACK OF ANY STEERING MECHANISM.

YES, THIS SLED IS TRULY A HAZARD TO LIFE AND LIMB.

WHEEE OOMPH! EEEEE

BOY, IS IT COLD! CAN'T WE TURN THE HEAT UP?

HEAT IS EXPENSIVE, CALVIN. JUST PUT ON A SWEATER.

LOOK, THE THERMOSTAT GOES ALL THE WAY UP TO 90 DEGREES! WE COULD BE SITTING AROUND IN OUR SHORTS!

LEAVE THE THERMOSTAT ALONE, CALVIN.

I CAN ALMOST SEE MY BREATH. I'LL JUST CRANK IT UP TO 75, OK?

I SAID DON'T TOUCH IT!

GEE, MY HANDS ARE SO NUMB, I CAN'T MOVE THE SWITCH. GUESS I'LL PUT ON A SWEATER.

OOH, YOU LOOK COLD, CALVIN! THERE'S A FIRE MADE. WHY DON'T YOU GO WARM UP?

OH BOY!

NOTHING BEATS SITTING BY A ROARING FIRE AFTER YOU'VE BEEN OUT IN THE COLD.

OF COURSE, SOME PEOPLE SAY WHY BOTHER GOING OUTSIDE FIRST?

CALVIN, I HOPE YOU TOOK YOUR BOOTS OFF BEFORE YOU WALKED ACROSS THE FLOOR.

OF COURSE I DID! YOU DON'T NEED TO TELL ME ALL THE TIME!

GIVEN ANY MORE THOUGHT TO THAT BACKYARD SKI LIFT PROPOSAL OF MINE?

OH, YES. LOTS.

HOBBES IS ALWAYS A LITTLE LOOPY WHEN HE COMES OUT OF THE DRYER.

WHATCHA DOIN'?

I'M WRITING MY AUTOBIOGRAPHY.

BUT YOU'RE JUST SIX YEARS OLD.

I'VE ONLY GOT ONE SHEET OF PAPER.

HI, HOBBES. ARE YOU READING THAT BOOK I GAVE YOU?

YES. IT'S VERY GOOD.

YOU LIKE IT?

SURE. I THINK IT'S...

WAIT A MINUTE.

WOULD YOU MIND WRITING IT IN TWO PAGES FOR ME BY TOMORROW MORNING?

MOM, WAS I ADOPTED?

NO, WHY DO YOU ASK?

ARE YOU PLANNING TO PUT ME TO WORK IN A CANNERY FOR 14 HOURS A DAY WHEN I TURN SEVEN?

OF COURSE NOT!

YOU'RE NOT JUST FATTENING ME UP TO EAT ME, ARE YOU?

GOOD HEAVENS, CALVIN! WHO PUT ALL THESE RIDICULOUS IDEAS IN YOUR HEAD?!?

THAT'S RIGHT. "RIDICULOUS IDEAS" SHE CALLED THEM.

OH, SURE, YOU THINK YOUR MOM'S GOING TO TELL *YOU*?

—WHIFFFFF...

WHIFF
WHIFF
WHIFF
WHIFF
WHIFF

FOR ALL THAT PREPARATION, YOU SURE ARE A LOUSY SHOT!

GO AHEAD DOWN. YOU'LL MISS ALL THOSE TREES.

YOU CAN DO IT. YOU'LL STOP BEFORE YOU GO OVER THAT LEDGE AT THE BOTTOM.

YOU WON'T GO INTO THAT POND. BESIDES, THE ICE IS PROBABLY REAL THICK ANYWAY. GO AHEAD DOWN.

MY BRAIN IS TRYING TO KILL ME.

GALOSH
GALOSH
GALOSH

197

I CALLED SUSIE A BOOGER-BRAIN AFTER SCHOOL, AND SHE WENT HOME CRYING.

GOODNESS, WHY'D YOU DO *THAT*?

I DUNNO. I WAS JUST TEASING.

IT SOUNDS LIKE YOU HURT HER FEELINGS.

I DIDN'T MEAN FOR HER TO TAKE THE INSULT *PERSONALLY!*

✳SNIFF✳ THAT STUPID CALVIN. WHY DOES HE CALL ME NAMES FOR NO REASON? IT'S JUST MEAN.

I WISH I HAD A HUNDRED FRIENDS. *THEN* I WOULDN'T CARE. I'D SAY, "WHO NEEDS *YOU*, CALVIN? I'VE GOT A HUNDRED OTHER FRIENDS!"

THEN MY HUNDRED FRIENDS AND I WOULD GO DO SOMETHING FUN, AND LEAVE CALVIN ALL ALONE! HA!

...AND AS LONG AS I'M DREAMING, I'D LIKE A PONY.

I FEEL BAD THAT I CALLED SUSIE NAMES AND HURT HER FEELINGS.

I'M SORRY I DID IT.

MAYBE YOU SHOULD APOLOGIZE TO HER.

I KEEP HOPING THERE'S A LESS OBVIOUS SOLUTION.

"STICKS AND STONES MAY BREAK MY BONES, BUT WORDS WILL NEVER HURT ME."

YEAH, RIGHT.

UM... HI, SUSIE.. I... UH... WELL...

GET LOST, CALVIN. YOU'RE MEAN.

DON'T WALK AWAY! I'M TRYING TO APOLOGIZE, YOU DUMB NOODLELOAF!

SLAP

SUSIE, I'M SORRY I CALLED YOU NAMES. I DIDN'T MEAN TO HURT YOUR FEELINGS.

WELL, YOU *DID* HURT MY FEELINGS, BUT I ACCEPT YOUR APOLOGY. THANK YOU.

OH BOY, THANK GOODNESS I GOT *THAT* OVER WITH!

...ON SECOND THOUGHT, LET'S SEE YOU GROVEL A LITTLE BIT!

WELL, WELL! IT'S AN INVITATION TO SUSIE DERKINS' BIRTHDAY PARTY. HOW NICE.

SUSIE INVITED *YOU*? WHAT ABOUT ME? DOES IT SAY ME TOO?

NO, IT DOESN'T SAY ANYTHING ABOUT YOU.

SHE MUST HAVE MAILED MY INVITATION SEPARATELY. SHE PROBABLY WANTED TO INSURE IT SO SHE'LL KNOW IT DIDN'T GET LOST. SOMETIMES THOSE TAKE LONGER.

I'LL HAVE TO SIGN FOR IT AND ALL. I'M SURE SHE'S TAKING NO CHANCES WITH MINE.

OH WAIT. ON THE BACK IT SAYS, "YOU CAN BRING THAT STUPID KID YOU HANG AROUND WITH, IF YOU MUST."

WE GET TO GO TO A BIRTHDAY PARTY!

THAT STUPID SUSIE.

BALLOONS, CAKE, PRESENTS... OH BOY!

SHE WON'T BE GETTING A VERY BIG PRESENT FROM *ME*, THAT'S FOR SURE.

I BET WE'LL PLAY GAMES, TOO! IT WILL BE FUN!

HMPH.

MAYBE WE'LL PLAY "SPIN THE BOTTLE"!

OH GET REAL!

I'LL MAKE A LIST OF POSSIBLE GIFTS FOR SUSIE'S BIRTHDAY. WHAT SHOULD WE GIVE HER?

HOW ABOUT A MOUTH FULL OF BROKEN TEETH? THAT'S WHAT *I'D* LIKE TO GIVE HER.

OH, DON'T BE SO CRANKY.

I THINK WE SHOULD GET HER A CAN OF TUNA FISH.

TUNA FISH? WHY WOULD SHE WANT *THAT*?

WELL, MAYBE SHE WOULDN'T, AND WE COULD OFFER TO TAKE IT BACK.....AND BORROW SOME BREAD, A LITTLE MAYO ...

RIGHT, HOBBES.

SUSIE'S HOUSE IS THE NEXT ONE UP.

THIS IS OUR LAST CHANCE TO NOT SHOW UP AND HAVE A NEW BIKE HORN.

HI, SUSIE. HAPPY BIRTHDAY!

HELLO, CALVIN. THANKS FOR COMING.

OH, LOOK AT YOUR STUFFED TIGER! HE'S WEARING A TIE!

HE'S JUST *ADORABLE!*

OK, YOU WERE RIGHT. GIRLS FLIP FOR TIES. YOU CAN STOP WINKING AT ME.

C'MON IN.

OK, EVERYONE, THE IDEA OF A SCAVENGER HUNT IS TO BRING BACK AS MANY OF THESE ITEMS AS YOU CAN IN HALF AN HOUR. LET'S GO!

QUICK, HOBBES, WHAT'S THE FIRST ITEM?

AN OLD LICENSE PLATE.

GREAT! I SAW ONE ON THE WAY OVER! C'MON!

GOOD THING I ALWAYS CARRY A SWISS ARMY KNIFE. NOBODY'S COMING, RIGHT?

IS THIS GAME LEGAL?

HERE'S A PAPER PLATE FOR THE BIRTHDAY CAKE, CALVIN.

THANK YOU.

I HOPE IT'S GOOD. I HATE IT WHEN THE BIRTHDAY KID CHOOSES SOMETHING GROSS LIKE COCONUT.

YOU DON'T HAVE TO WORRY. IT'S CHOCOLATE.

OH, GOOD. DID YOU SEE IT?

HEY! WHO CUT A PIECE OF MY CAKE ALREADY?! I DIDN'T EVEN GET TO BLOW OUT THE CANDLES!!

IT'S NICE AND MOIST, TOO.

GLAD YOU BOTH COULD COME. THANK YOU FOR THE NICE PRESENT. GOOD-BYE.

*

MOM MAY NOT WANT THIS PIECE OF CAKE AND ICE CREAM WE'RE BRINGING HER.

HEY! IT SNOWED LAST NIGHT!

OH, BOY! LOOK AT IT ALL! THEY'LL HAVE TO CLOSE THE SCHOOLS!

SNOW EVERYWHERE! IT MUST BE WAIST DEEP!

UNFORTUNATELY, THAT'S A RELATIVE MEASURE.

WHAT'S THE TEACHER HANDING OUT?

OUR REPORT CARDS.

OUR REPORT CARDS?

YOU KNOW, OUR GRADES.

GRADES? WE'RE BEING GRADED?

OF COURSE, DUMMY. WHAT DID YOU THINK?

DON'T WE EVEN GET A FEW PRACTICE SEMESTERS?

I BROUGHT MY REPORT CARD HOME, DAD.

WELL! LET'S SEE IT!

REMEMBER HOW YOU ONCE TOLD ME IT DIDN'T MATTER WHAT GRADES I GOT...

... JUST SO LONG AS I TRIED MY HARDEST. RIGHT?

WELL YOU COULD CERTAINLY BE TRYING HARDER THAN *THIS!*

SO YOU ADMIT YOU WERE LYING?

DAD SAYS MY REPORT CARD SHOWS THAT NOT ENOUGH TIME IS BEING SPENT ON MY HOMEWORK.

SO FROM DINNER TILL BED IS NOW DESIGNATED AS "HOMEWORK TIME."

I DON'T THINK THAT'S FAIR!

IF IT DOESN'T TAKE THAT LONG TO DO, WHY SHOULD I HAVE TO STAY IN MY ROOM ALL THAT TIME?

YEAH. CAN *I* HELP IT I'M SO FAST?

CAN I HAVE SOME CLAY? HELP YOURSELF. THIS STUFF'S IMPOSSIBLE TO WORK WITH.

THANKS. I'VE GOT A PRETTY GOOD BOWL OR SOMETHING GOING HERE.

IT STARTED OUT AS A PHANTOM JET, BUT IT SORT OF SQUASHED, SO NOW I THINK IT'S A BOWL.

MMM. THAT'S VERY GOOD. YEAH, I'M REAL PLEASED WITH IT.

WATTERSON

UH OH. THERE'S A DINOSAUR IN THE KITCHEN.

YAARRGH

WELL IF YOU SEE CALVIN ANYWHERE, TELL HIM IT'S ALMOST TIME FOR DINNER.

WATTERSON

I'D INVITE YOU, BUT NO DINOSAURS ARE ALLOWED AT THE DINNER TABLE.

HA. DINOSAURS EAT ANYWHERE THEY WANT.

LET'S GO, CALVIN. TIME FOR YOUR BATH.

I'M NOT TAKING BATHS ANYMORE. I HATE THEM.

OH? AND HOW ARE YOU GOING TO STAY CLEAN?

EASY.

WATTERSON

EITHER HE'S PLAYING CLASSICAL MUSIC AT 78 RPM, OR I'M STILL DREAMING.

FIRST THING TOMORROW MORNING, I'M CALLING THE ORPHANAGE.

WHERE DO WE KEEP ALL OUR CHAINSAWS, MOM?

WE DON'T HAVE ANY CHAINSAWS, CALVIN.

WE DON'T? NOT ANY?

NOPE.

HOW AM I EVER GOING TO LEARN HOW TO JUGGLE?

THE GIANT AMOEBA SLIDES ALONG THE KITCHEN FLOOR.

EXTENDING A CYTOPLASMIC PSEUDOPOD, THE PROTOZOAN ENGULFS A PACKAGE OF OATMEAL COOKIES.

CRUNCH CRUNCH

NICE TRY. PUT THEM BACK.

THE MAJESTIC EAGLE CIRCLES SLOWLY IN THE CLOUDS.

WITH EYES SO SHARP HE CAN SPOT MOVEMENT A MILE BELOW, HE SIGHTS HIS PREY AND DIVES!

REACHING SPEEDS OF MORE THAN 100 MPH, HIS UNWARY PRIZE WILL NEVER KNOW WHAT HIT IT!

WAKE UP, DAD! IT'S SATURDAY!

ZZ... WHA?

Calvin and Hobbes

by WATTERSON

HERE IS SUCCESSFUL MR. JONES. HE LIVES IN A 5-ACRE HOME IN A WEALTHY SUBURB. HERE IS HIS NEW MERCEDES IN THE DRIVEWAY.

IT'S ANYONE'S GUESS AS TO HOW MUCH LONGER MR. JONES CAN MEET HIS MONTHLY FINANCE CHARGES.

HERE COMES MR. JONES OUT OF HIS ATTRACTIVE SUBURBAN HOME. HE HOPS IN HIS RED SPORTS CAR.

OFF HE GOES TO WORK. 80...90... 100 MILES AN HOUR!

... ALONG THE EDGE OF THE GRAND CANYON !!

SUDDENLY, HIS STEERING LOCKS AND HIS BRAKES FAIL! HE CAREENS OVER THE EDGE! OH NO! DOWN HE GOES!

HIS ONLY HOPE IS TO CLIMB OUT THE SUN ROOF AND JUMP! MAYBE, JUST MAYBE, HE CAN GRAB A BRANCH AND SAVE HIMSELF! HE UNWINDS THE SUN ROOF! CAN HE MAKE IT ??

NO! THE CAR EXPLODES IN MID-AIR, PROPELLING MILLIONS OF TINY SHARDS INTO THE STRATOSPHERE! *KABLOOIE!*

THE NEIGHBORS HEAR THE BOOM ECHOING ACROSS THE CANYON. THEY PILE INTO A MINI-VAN TO INVESTIGATE! WHAT WILL HAPPEN TO *THEM*?

213

HOW COME IT DOESN'T TAKE YOU AS LONG AS MOM TO VACUUM THE HOUSE?

MAYBE I'M MORE EFFICIENT.

MAYBE YOU DON'T DO AS GOOD A JOB.

WHY DON'T YOU GO FIND SOMETHING TO DO, MR. CRITIC?

OK, CAN I TAKE THIS DUST BALL IN FOR "SHOW AND TELL" TOMORROW?

CALVIN, THIS DUST BALL IS GOING TO BE OUR LITTLE SECRET, ALL RIGHT?

AAACCK! LOOK AT THIS THING! DEAR, I THOUGHT YOU *DID* THIS ROOM!

I'VE BEEN IN THE WATER ABOUT 20 MINUTES. LOOK AT MY FINGERS.

THEY'RE ALL WRINKLED!

SO ARE MY TOES!

PRETTY NEAT, HUH?

"BIG PINK RAISIN DISCOVERED IN TUB -- BOY'S WHEREABOUTS UNKNOWN!"

AAUUGH!

FOR THE NEXT 60 SECONDS, I WILL CONDUCT A TEST OF MY EMERGENCY BROADCAST EQUIPMENT.

AAAAAAH GHHH HHH

HAD THIS BEEN A REAL EMERGENCY, THE SCREAM YOU JUST HEARD WOULD HAVE BEEN FOLLOWED BY LOTS MORE JUST LIKE IT. THIS CONCLUDES MY...

OH, SOMEDAY WHEN THE HOUSE CAVES IN, SHE'LL THANK ME. MARK MY WORDS.

OH, MOM, I NEED SOME CRISCO FOR SCHOOL TODAY!

SHORTENING? HONESTLY, CALVIN, I WISH YOU'D REMEMBER THESE THINGS THE NIGHT BEFORE. NOW HURRY UP AND GET READY.

RIGHT.

HERE'S THE CRISCO BACK. THANKS.

YOU PUT IT IN YOUR HAIR??

GET BACK HERE! YOU'RE NOT GOING TO SCHOOL LIKE THAT!

AW C'MON, MOM! IT'S CLASS PICTURE DAY!

WHAT'S WITH YOUR HAIR?

I TOLD MOM I'M GETTING MY SCHOOL PICTURE TAKEN TODAY, AND SHE MADE ME COMB OUT THE CRISCO I PUT IN MY HAIR. NOW I LOOK LIKE A MORON.

THAT'S TRUE. YOU DO.

WELL DON'T JUST STAND THERE! THINK OF SOMETHING! WHAT CAN I DO?

THERE. MUCH BETTER!

WHAT'D YOU DO? IS IT COOL? IS IT NEW WAVE? GEE, I WISH I HAD A MIRROR...

THE BUS IS GOING TO BE HERE ANY MINUTE. YOU'RE SURE YOU FIXED MY HAIR SO IT LOOKS OK?

IT LOOKS GREAT. TRY NOT TO MUSS IT UP.

YOU'RE NOT KIDDING ME, ARE YOU? THIS REALLY LOOKS GOOD?

TRUST ME. YOU LOOK LIKE ... LIKE...

"... ASTRO BOY."

ALL RIGHT! I CAN'T WAIT TO GET MY PICTURE TAKEN NOW!

CALVIN! WHAT DID YOU DO TO YOUR HAIR?? DON'T YOU KNOW WE HAVE OUR PICTURES TAKEN TODAY?

OF COURSE, SILLY. THAT'S WHY I DID IT. IT'S CRISCO.

DOES YOUR MOM KNOW YOU LOOK LIKE THAT?

SORT OF. HOBBES FIXED ME UP A LITTLE AT THE BUS STOP.

WOW. I WISH *I* HAD SOME CRISCO.

WAIT TILL MOM SENDS MY PICTURE TO GRANDMA!

OK, KID, SIT UP STRAIGHT ON THE STOOL AND LOOK RIGHT AT ME. THAT'S IT.

ARE YOU READY TO TAKE MY PICTURE? SHOULD I TAKE OFF MY SHIRT NOW?

KID, WHAT ARE...? DON'T TAKE OFF YOUR SHIRT!!

SEE? I PAINTED A FACE ON MY STOMACH.

KID, PUT YOUR SHIRT BACK ON.

BUT LOOK! WHEN I BREATHE OUT, THE FACE CHANGES! SEE? OK, TAKE ONE QUICK!

LOOK, HOBBES, I GOT MY SCHOOL PICTURES BACK.

LOOK AT YOU! HA HA HA! LOOK AT YOUR HAIR! HEE HEE! THESE ARE GREAT!

AREN'T THEY, THOUGH?

HEE HEE HEE! LOOK AT THIS ONE! WHAT AN EXPRESSION! HOO HOO HOO! HA HA!

YEAH, SEE HOW I GOT MY ONE EYE TO ROLL BACK?

HA HA HA! YOUR MOTHER'S GOING TO GO INTO CONNIPTIONS, OF COURSE..

OH, C'MON. YEARS FROM NOW, THINK OF THE MEMORIES THESE WILL BRING.

Calvin and Hobbes

by WATTERSON

GLIK
GLIK
GLIK

OH NO! WHAT HAVE I DONE?!?

THE HUMAN BODY IS 80% WATER. LITTLE DID CALVIN REALIZE HOW CRITICAL IT IS TO MAINTAIN THAT!

NOW IT'S TOO LATE! BY DRINKING THAT EXTRA GLASS OF WATER, CALVIN HAS UPSET THAT PRECIOUS BALANCE! HE IS NOW **90%** WATER!

EVERYTHING SOLID IN CALVIN'S BODY BEGINS TO DISSOLVE!

HE IS BECOMING A LIQUID!!

HIS ONLY HOPE IS SOMEHOW TO GET TO AN ICEBOX AND FREEZE HIMSELF SOLID UNTIL HE CAN GET PROPER MEDICAL ATTENTION!

UNFORTUNATELY, AS A LIQUID, CALVIN CAN ONLY RUN DOWNHILL! CAN HE MAKE IT? CAN HE MAKE IT??

I DON'T THINK I'M GONNA MAKE IT.

THERE'S A GAS STATION UP AHEAD. JUST HOLD ON.

DIDN'T I TELL YOU NOT TO DRINK SO MUCH BEFORE WE LEFT?!

CALVIN, ALL WE WANT IS FOR YOU TO STUDY AND DO YOUR BEST IN SCHOOL. EDUCATION IS VERY IMPORTANT.

THAT'S WHY THIS AMNESIA GAME HAS TO STOP. NO MORE "FORGETTING" TO DO YOUR HOMEWORK.

OK?

OK, MISTER.

OK?

...UH, **DAD**. RIGHT, DAD. YOU GOT IT.

I'M GLAD TO SEE YOU'RE DOING YOUR HOMEWORK. HOW IS YOUR MATH CLASS GOING NOW?

UM... I'M DOING GREAT.

HOW GREAT?

REAL GREAT.

HAVE YOU BEEN PASSING ALL YOUR QUIZZES?

I DIDN'T SAY PHENOMENAL.

RING RING

RING RING

RI---

IT'S NEVER FOR ME AND I HATE TAKING MESSAGES.

Calvin and Hobbes

by WATTERSON

I'M HOME!

WAAA
AAUUGH!

I THOUGHT THAT AFTER SEVEN BORING HOURS AT SCHOOL, YOU MIGHT APPRECIATE ONE MOMENT OF PURE, ABJECT TERROR.

LET ME UP TO GET MY BAT AND I'LL THANK YOU.

HOBBES, LOOK! THERE'S A LITTLE RACCOON ON THE GROUND.

IS IT ALIVE?

I THINK SO, BUT HE'S HURT. SEE, HE'S HARDLY BREATHING.

BETTER NOT TOUCH HIM IF HE'S HURT.

YEAH. YOU WAIT HERE AND GUARD HIM. I'LL RUN AND GET MOM.

I SURE HOPE SHE CAN HELP.

OF COURSE SHE CAN! YOU DON'T GET TO BE MOM IF YOU CAN'T FIX EVERYTHING JUST RIGHT.

THERE'S HOBBES GUARDING HIM, MOM. THE LITTLE RACCOON'S RIGHT OVER THERE!

OOH, CALVIN, I DON'T KNOW IF WE CAN SAVE HIM. HE LOOKS PRETTY BAD. GO GET A SHOE BOX AND A CLEAN DISH TOWEL.

RIGHT!

I DON'T THINK THIS POOR LITTLE GUY IS GOING TO MAKE IT, HOBBES. (SIGH) I HATE IT WHEN THESE THINGS HAPPEN.

...YOU CAN TELL I'M UPSET WHEN I START TALKING TO *YOU*...

WELL, I GOT HIM IN THE SHOE BOX. I GUESS ALL WE CAN DO IS KEEP HIM WARM AND SAFE.

WE'LL KEEP HIM IN THE GARAGE, AND PUT OUT SOME WATER AND FOOD.

I READ IN A BOOK THAT RACCOONS WILL EAT JUST ABOUT ANYTHING.

CHANCES ARE, I'LL BE HAPPY TO DONATE MOST OF MY DINNER.

CALVIN, YOU DON'T EVEN KNOW WHAT WE'RE HAVING.

THIS IS WHERE DAD BURIED THE LITTLE RACCOON.

I DIDN'T EVEN KNOW HE EXISTED A FEW DAYS AGO AND NOW HE'S GONE FOREVER. IT'S LIKE I FOUND HIM FOR NO REASON. I HAD TO SAY GOOD-BYE AS SOON AS I SAID HELLO.

STILL... IN A SAD, AWFUL, TERRIBLE WAY, I'M HAPPY I MET HIM.

SNIFF

WHAT A STUPID WORLD.

YOU KNOW, HOBBES, I CAN'T FIGURE OUT THIS DEATH STUFF.

WHY DID THAT LITTLE RACCOON HAVE TO DIE? HE DIDN'T DO ANYTHING WRONG.

HE WAS JUST LITTLE! WHAT'S THE POINT OF PUTTING HIM HERE AND TAKING HIM BACK SO SOON?!?

IT'S EITHER MEAN OR IT'S ARBITRARY, AND EITHER WAY I'VE GOT THE HEEBIE-JEEBIES.

WHY IS IT ALWAYS NIGHT WHEN WE TALK ABOUT THESE THINGS?

MOM SAYS DEATH IS AS NATURAL AS BIRTH, AND IT'S ALL PART OF THE LIFE CYCLE.

SHE SAYS WE DON'T REALLY UNDERSTAND IT, BUT THERE ARE MANY THINGS WE DON'T UNDERSTAND, AND WE JUST HAVE TO DO THE BEST WE CAN WITH THE KNOWLEDGE WE HAVE.

I GUESS THAT MAKES SENSE.

...BUT DON'T *YOU* GO ANYWHERE.

DON'T WORRY.

HEY! WHAT HAPPENED TO THE TREES HERE? WHO CLEARED OUT THE WOODS?

THERE USED TO BE LOTS OF ANIMALS IN THESE WOODS! NOW IT'S A MUD PIT!

THIS SIGN SAYS, "FUTURE SITE OF SHADY ACRES CONDOMINIUMS."

ANIMALS CAN'T AFFORD CONDOS!

"SHADY ACRES"? THE ONLY SHADE *I* SEE IS FROM THAT BULLDOZER.

WHERE ARE ALL THE ANIMALS SUPPOSED TO LIVE NOW THAT THEY CUT DOWN THESE WOODS TO PUT IN HOUSES??

BY GOLLY, HOW WOULD *PEOPLE* LIKE IT IF ANIMALS BULLDOZED A SUBURB AND PUT IN NEW *TREES*?!?

NO GOOD. THEY DIDN'T LEAVE THE KEYS.

IT TOOK HUNDREDS OF YEARS FOR THESE WOODS TO GROW, AND THEY LEVELED IT IN A WEEK. IT'S GONE.

AFTER THEY BUILD NEW HOUSES HERE, THEY'LL HAVE TO WIDEN THE ROADS AND PUT UP GAS STATIONS, AND PRETTY SOON THIS WHOLE AREA WILL JUST BE A BIG STRIP.

EVENTUALLY THERE WON'T BE A NICE SPOT LEFT ANYWHERE.

I WONDER IF YOU CAN REFUSE TO INHERIT THE WORLD.

I THINK IF YOU'RE BORN, IT'S TOO LATE.

HOBBES, WANT TO SEE MY TRANSMOGRIFIER?

I DIDN'T KNOW YOU HAD A TRANSMOGRIFIER.

I JUST GOT IT.

YOU STEP INTO THIS CHAMBER, SET THE APPROPRIATE DIALS, AND IT TURNS YOU INTO WHATEVER YOU'D LIKE TO BE.

TRANSMOG-RIFIER

IT'S AMAZING WHAT THEY DO WITH CORRUGATED CARDBOARD THESE DAYS.

ISN'T IT?

THIS TRANSMOGRIFIER WILL TURN YOU INTO ANYTHING AT ALL.

ALL YOU DO IS SET THIS INDICATOR, AND THE MACHINE AUTOMATICALLY RESTRUCTURES YOUR CHEMICAL CONFIGURATION. YOU CAN BE AN EEL, A BABOON, A GIANT BUG, OR A DINOSAUR.

WHAT IF YOU WANT TO BE SOMETHING ELSE?

I LEFT SOME ROOM. JUST WRITE IT ON THE SIDE.

WELL, WHAT DO YOU SAY? WOULD YOU LIKE TO BE TRANSMOGRIFIED?

I DON'T THINK SO. BEING A TIGER IS MY AREA OF EXPERTISE.

DON'T BE SCARED. THE PROCESS IS INSTANTANEOUS AND COMPLETELY PAINLESS.

JUST THINK! WITH THE PUSH OF A BUTTON, YOU COULD BE A 500-STORY GASTROPOD — A SLUG THE SIZE OF THE CHRYSLER BUILDING!

GOSH, HOW CAN I REFUSE?

WELL IF YOU DON'T LIKE THAT, BE SOMETHING ELSE! I DON'T CARE!

SO CALVIN, WHAT'S IT LIKE TO BE A TIGER NOW?

KINDA FUZZY, BUT NOT THAT DIFFERENT.

SO! WHAT DO YOU WANT TO TALK ABOUT?

DO WE EAT SOON?

HI, MOM! WILL YOU MAKE HOBBES AND ME A BIG TUNA SANDWICH?

I THOUGHT YOU HATED TUNA FISH.

NOT ANYMORE. I'M A TIGER NOW.

I THOUGHT HOBBES WAS YOUR TIGER.

NOW I'M ONE TOO. I TRANSMOGRIFIED.

OH, I SEE.

MY, SHE'S TAKING THIS WELL. BUT THE STRAIN WILL SURELY CRACK HER SOON.

I'M HOME!

HI, DAD. NOTICE ANYTHING DIFFERENT ABOUT ME?

UH... NEW HAIRCUT?

GEEZ, DID YOU GO BLIND?? I'M A TIGER!

OH, I THOUGHT YOU MEANT BESIDES THAT. CALVIN, YOUR DAD'S VERY TIRED, AND...

HOPE YOU WANT TUNA FOR DINNER, DEAR...

231

CALVIN and HOBBES

by WATERSON

Look, Jane. See Spot.
See Spot run.
Run, Spot, run.
Jane sees Spot run.

RRINNGGG!

RECESS IS OVER!

R-R-RIPP!

SNAG

OH NO!

WHY IS IT YOU ALWAYS RIP YOUR PANTS ON THE DAY EVERYONE HAS TO DEMONSTRATE A MATH PROBLEM AT THE CHALKBOARD?

WATTERSON

I CAN'T BELIEVE I RIPPED MY PANTS! RECESS IS OVER. I'M SUPPOSED TO BE BACK IN CLASS!

I CAN'T GO IN LIKE THIS! WHAT AM I GOING TO DO??

...OF ALL THE DAYS TO WEAR THE UNDERPANTS WITH THE LITTLE ROCKET SHIPS...

WATTERSON

LOOK AT THE SIZE OF THIS RIP! MAYBE I CAN PULL MY SHIRT DOWN OVER IT.

NO, THAT DOESN'T WORK. MAYBE I CAN TUCK MY SHIRT INTO THE HOLE. ..NOPE..

MAYBE I CAN STICK THE RIPPED PART UNDER MY BELT. NO, THAT DOESN'T WORK EITHER.

WATTERSON

MAYBE I CAN SCOOT AROUND ON MY REAR THE REST OF THE DAY.

PLEASE DON'T LET THE TEACHER CALL ON ME! DON'T MAKE ME GO TO THE BOARD IN MY RIPPED PANTS!

ANYONE BUT ME! JUST LET HER CALL ON SOMEONE ELSE! PLEASE DON'T EMBARRASS ME IN FRONT OF THE WHOLE CLASS!

CALVIN, WOULD YOU DO THE NEXT PROBLEM AT THE BOARD?

SO MUCH FOR MY EVER JOINING THE CLERGY.

CALVIN, WILL YOU DO THE NEXT PROBLEM AT THE BOARD, PLEASE?

NO.

WHY NOT?

FRANKLY, I'D RATHER NOT SAY.

OH, YOU WOULDN'T?

IT'S A PERSONAL MATTER.

YOU'RE GOING TO HAVE TO DO BETTER THAN *THAT*.

DO THE WORDS "COMPLETE PANDEMONIUM" STRIKE TERROR IN YOUR HEART?

SO YOUR TEACHER DIDN'T KNOW YOU'D RIPPED YOUR PANTS, AND SHE MADE YOU DO A PROBLEM AT THE CHALKBOARD?

THAT SUMS IT UP.

HOW AWFUL! WHAT DID YOU DO.??

I DIDN'T HAVE A CHOICE. I MOONED THE WHOLE CLASS.

THAT'S WHY YOU'RE HOME EARLY?

THREE TEACHERS AND THE PRINCIPAL COULDN'T RESTORE ORDER.

CALVIN and HOBBES
by WATTERSON

"DURING EMERGENCY LANDING, REPLACE DINNER TRAY AND BRING SEAT TO UPRIGHT POSITION. EXTINGUISH ALL SMOKING MATERIALS."

"...INCLUDING SPACECRAFT, IF POSSIBLE."

OUT OF FUEL, THE COURAGEOUS SPACEMAN SPIFF IS FORCED TO LAND ON THE DISTANT PLANET ZOK!

THE VALIANT EXPLORER SURVEYS THE ZOKKIAN LANDSCAPE. WHO KNOWS WHAT DANGERS LIE HIDDEN IN THE CRATERED TERRAIN?

UNDAUNTED, SPIFF SETS OUT TO FIND HELP!

MILES LATER, IT IS EVIDENT THE PLANET IS COMPLETELY UNINHABITED!

OUR HERO IS MAROONED ON A LIFELESS PLANET! ALONE ON AN ALIEN WORLD!

ALONE... ALL ALONE...

!

DARN IT, WHY DOESN'T ANYONE EVER *TELL* ME WHEN THE LUNCH BELL RINGS?

SUSIE, WHERE'S MISS WORMWOOD? WHO'S THAT LADY AT HER DESK?

MISS WORMWOOD'S SICK. THAT'S OUR SUBSTITUTE TEACHER.

A SUBSTITUTE?

LET'S SEE YOUR TEACHING CERTIFICATE, LADY!

GOOD MORNING, CLASS. I'LL BE YOUR SUBSTITUTE TEACHER TODAY.

MISS WORMWOOD LEFT ME INSTRUCTIONS AS TO WHAT WE NEED TO GO OVER, SO WE SHOULDN'T HAVE ANY PROBLEMS.

OH WAIT, HERE'S A NOTE SHE ADDED. JUST A SECOND...

OK, WHICH ONE OF YOU IS CALVIN?

NOT ME!

WE HAD A SUBSTITUTE TEACHER IN SCHOOL TODAY.

DID YOU LIKE HER?

SHE WAS OK, I GUESS.

YOU "GUESS"?

IT'S HARD TO SAY.

SHE WENT HOME AT NOON.

Mr. Jones lives 50 miles away from you. You both leave home at 5:00 and drive toward each other.

Mr. Jones travels at 35 mph., and you drive at 40 mph. At what time will you pass Mr. Jones on the road?

GIVEN THE TRAFFIC AROUND HERE AT 5:00, WHO KNOWS?

I ALWAYS CATCH THESE TRICK QUESTIONS.

I'VE GOT A SCHEME TO GET US SOME MONEY.

OH BOY.

SEE? I SNEAKED ALL THESE KERNELS OF CORN OFF MY DINNER PLATE TONIGHT.

HOW IS THAT GOING TO GET US MONEY?

EASY. I JUST STICK THEM UNDER MY PILLOW.

WITH ANY LUCK, THE TOOTH FAIRY WON'T KNOW THEY'RE FAKES UNTIL IT'S TOO LATE!

DAD, HOW DO PEOPLE MAKE BABIES?

MOST PEOPLE JUST GO TO SEARS, BUY THE KIT, AND FOLLOW THE ASSEMBLY INSTRUCTIONS.

I CAME FROM SEARS??

NO, YOU WERE A BLUE LIGHT SPECIAL AT K MART. ALMOST AS GOOD, AND A LOT CHEAPER.

AAUU GHHH!

DEAR, WHAT ARE YOU TELLING CALVIN NOW?!

I'VE GOT TO GIVE A 5-MINUTE ORAL REPORT IN SCHOOL ON THURSDAY.

WE'RE SUPPOSED TO RESEARCH OUR SUBJECT, WRITE IT UP, AND PRESENT IT TO THE CLASS WITH A VISUAL AID.

THAT'S A BIG ASSIGNMENT.

I'LL SAY. I HATE MY TEACHER.

SHE KNOWS WE'LL ALL DO IT ON THE LAST EVENING, BUT SHE GAVE US THREE DAYS TO WORRY ABOUT IT.

WHAT'S THE SUBJECT OF YOUR REPORT?

THE BRAIN.

WHAT DO YOU KNOW ABOUT BRAINS?

WELL, I SAW THIS MOVIE WHERE THEY KEPT THIS GUY'S BRAIN ALIVE IN A TANK OF WATER.

THEN A POWER SURGE MUTATED THE BRAIN, AND IT CRAWLED OUT AND TERRORIZED THE POPULACE.

THAT'S INFORMATIVE.

UNFORTUNATELY FOR MY REPORT, MOM CAUGHT ME, AND I DIDN'T GET TO SEE HOW IT ENDED.

I'VE GOT TO GIVE MY REPORT ON "THE BRAIN" AT SCHOOL TODAY.

SEE MY VISUAL AID? I COOKED SOME NOODLES AND PUT THEM IN A PAPER BAG. DOESN'T THAT LOOK LIKE BRAINS?

UGH.

WELL, I GUESS I'M ALL SET.

DID YOU WRITE YOUR REPORT YET?

NAH. I BORROWED MOM'S POCKET DICTIONARY. I'LL DO IT ON THE BUS.

MY FIVE-MINUTE REPORT IS ON "THE BRAIN."

OF COURSE, IT'S DIFFICULT TO EXPLAIN THE COMPLEXITIES OF THE BRAIN IN JUST FIVE MINUTES, BUT TO BEGIN, THE BRAIN IS PART OF THE CENTRAL NERVOUS SYSTEM.

I'LL PAUSE FOR A FEW MOMENTS, SO YOU ALL CAN FINISH WRITING THAT DOWN.

CALVIN!

POW! JAB! KICK! POW! POW!

RATTATATTATTATTA RATTATATTATTA

EEEEEEEEEE

BOOM!

PLEASE, PLEASE, PRETTY PLEASE?

NO. YOU SHOULD'VE SAVED SOME OF YOUR OWN HALLOWEEN CANDY.

HEY, CAN WE CHANGE THE CHANNEL NOW? I WANT TO WATCH SOMETHING ELSE.

MY SHOW'S NOT OVER YET.

AW C'MON! YOU SEE THIS PROGRAM ALL THE TIME! CAN'T WE WATCH MY SHOW FOR ONCE?

NO, I WAS HERE FIRST. PIPE DOWN. THIS IS A GOOD PART.

AARRGHH

I HATE NATIONAL GEOGRAPHIC ANIMAL SPECIALS.

Point A is twice as far from point C as point B is from A. If the distance from point B to point C is 5 inches, how far is point A from point C?

THE LIVING DEAD DON'T **NEED** TO SOLVE WORD PROBLEMS.

CALVIN THE ZOMBIE SEARCHES FOR FOOD.

HORRIBLY, THE UNDEAD FEED UPON THE LIVING!

...ALTHOUGH, IN A PINCH, A PBJ WILL DO, IF YOU EAT IT MESSILY ENOUGH.

"WHEN IN ROME..."

GKPTHH!
HEE HEE...
!

THPKK!
HEE HEE..

HEE HEE HOO HOO HA
HA HA HA
HA HO HO HO
HEE HEE HO

HEH HEH... OF COURSE, *REAL* ZOMBIES *NEVER* GET THE GIGGLES BY LOOKING AT EACH OTHER.

HEE HEE

OH NO! TOO MUCH BUBBLE BATH!

UH OH!

POP!

HOW ON EARTH DO YOU *DO* THIS??!

THESE THINGS JUST SEEM TO HAPPEN.

AAUUGHHHHHH

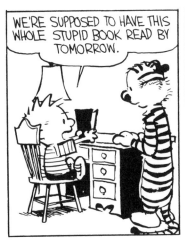

WE'RE SUPPOSED TO HAVE THIS WHOLE STUPID BOOK READ BY TOMORROW.

FLIP-IP-IP-IP-IP-IP!

THERE! IT'S GOOD TO GET *THAT* OUT OF THE WAY!

READING GOES FASTER IF YOU DON'T SWEAT COMPREHENSION.

WHERE'S THE FRISBEE?

AHOY! TOSS THE ROPE LADDER DOWN!

WHAT'S THE PASSWORD?

"TIGERS ARE MEAN! TIGERS ARE FIERCE! TIGERS HAVE TEETH AND CLAWS THAT PIERCE!"

"TIGERS ARE GREAT! THEY CAN'T BE BEAT! IF I WAS A TIGER, THAT WOULD BE NEAT!"

HE CAN CLIMB THE TREE WITHOUT THE LADDER, SO *HE* GOT TO MAKE UP THE PASSWORD.

GO ON, WHAT'S THE *THIRD* VERSE?

MOM, WHEN ARE YOU GOING SHOPPING NEXT?

I DON'T KNOW. WHY?

WE SEEM TO BE OUT OF GUN POWDER.

SHEESH, I DIDN'T EVEN *DO* IT YET.

NOW!

ARE YOU SURE THERE'S A CAREER TO BE MADE AS A "HUMAN DISCUS"?

WELL, WE GOTTA GET A BIGGER FIELD....

I TRIPPED A KID YESTERDAY, AND HE FELL IN THE MUD. IT WAS HILARIOUS.

AAUGH!

TRIP

PLOOP!

I DUNNO. THAT KIND OF HUMOR IS SO BROAD.

YOU DIDN'T DO IT RIGHT. C'MERE AND GIVE ME A HAND.

WHAT'S THIS? IT LOOKS GROSS.

IT'S A VEGETARIAN MEAL. IT'S GOOD FOR YOU.

VEGETARIAN?? YECCHH! I'M NOT A VEGETARIAN!

I'M A DESSERTARIAN.

251

TAKE YOUR HAT OFF AT THE DINNER TABLE, CALVIN.

HERE COMES THE HURRICANE.

YOU CUT YOUR HAIR!!

NO I DIDN'T. HOBBES DID.

WHY ON EARTH DID YOU CUT YOUR OWN HAIR?! LOOK AT YOU!

I SAID HOBBES CUT IT! YOU THINK I'D DO THIS??

...WELL, I DIDN'T!

SOME BARBER YOU ARE! MOM SAYS THERE'S NOTHING I CAN DO BUT WAIT FOR MY HAIR TO GROW BACK.

IN THE MEANTIME, I'VE GOT TO GO AROUND LOOKING LIKE I'VE GOT MANGE! I HOPE YOU'RE HAPPY.

HAPPY?! YOU STIFFED ME! WHERE'S MY EIGHT BUCKS?!

LOOK, I'M SORRY I GAVE YOU A BAD HAIRCUT. I DIDN'T MEAN TO.

A FAT LOT OF GOOD THAT DOES ME.

I CAN MAKE IT UP TO YOU. HONEST.

YEAH? HOW?

I BOUGHT A YELLOW MAGIC MARKER.

SEE, I'LL JUST DRAW SOME HAIR ON. THERE, IT'S LOOKING BETTER ALREADY.

REALLY? IS IT?

The End